The Light Eternal: J.M.W. Turner
by Jeremy Mark Robinson

Maurice Sendak and the Art of Children's Book Illustration
by L.M. Poole

Sex in Art: Pornography and Pleasure in Painting and Sculpture
by Cassidy Hughes

*Glorification: Religious Abstraction
In Renaissance and 20th Century Painting*
by Jeremy Mark Robinson

The Art of Andy Goldsworthy
by William Malpas

Andy Goldsworthy: Touching Nature
by William Malpas

Andy Goldsworthy In Close-Up
by William Malpas

The Art of Richard Long
by William Malpas

Constantin Brancusi: Sculpting the Essence of Things
by James Pearson

Alison Wilding: The Embrace of Sculpture
by Susan Quinnell

*The Erotic Object: Sexuality in Sculpture
From Prehistory to the Present Day*
by Susan Quinnell

*Land Art: A Complete Guide to Landscape, Environmental,
Earthworks, Nature, Sculpture and Installation Art*
by William Malpas

Land Art In Close-Up
by William Malpas

*Colourfield Painting: Minimal, Cool, Hard Edge, Serial
and Post-Painterly Abstract Art From the Sixties to the Present*
by Laura Garrard

REMBRANDT AND HIS WORKS

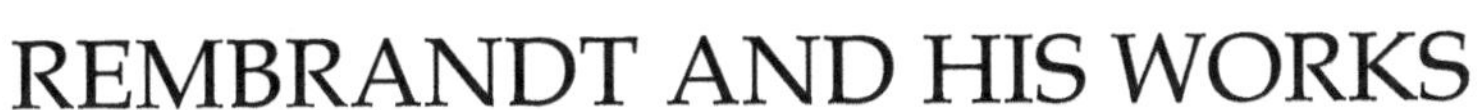

REMBRANDT AND HIS WORKS

COMPRISING

A SHORT ACCOUNT OF HIS LIFE;
WITH A CRITICAL EXAMINATION INTO HIS PRINCIPLES
AND PRACTICE OF DESIGN, LIGHT, SHADE, AND COLOUR.

BY
JOHN BURNET, F.R.S.

AUTHOR OF "PRACTICAL HINTS ON PAINTING."

CRESCENT MOON

First published 1901. This edition © 2018.

Printed and bound in the U.S.A.
Set in Book Antiqua 10 on 14pt.
Designed by Radiance Graphics.

British Library Cataloguing in Publication data

ISBN-13 9781861716323

CRESCENT MOON PUBLISHING
P.O. Box 1312, Maidstone, Kent, ME14 5XU
Great Britain, www.crmoon.com

CONTENTS

NOTE ON THE TEXT

The text is from *Rembrandt van Rijn* by John Burnet, published by
David Bogue, London, 1901.

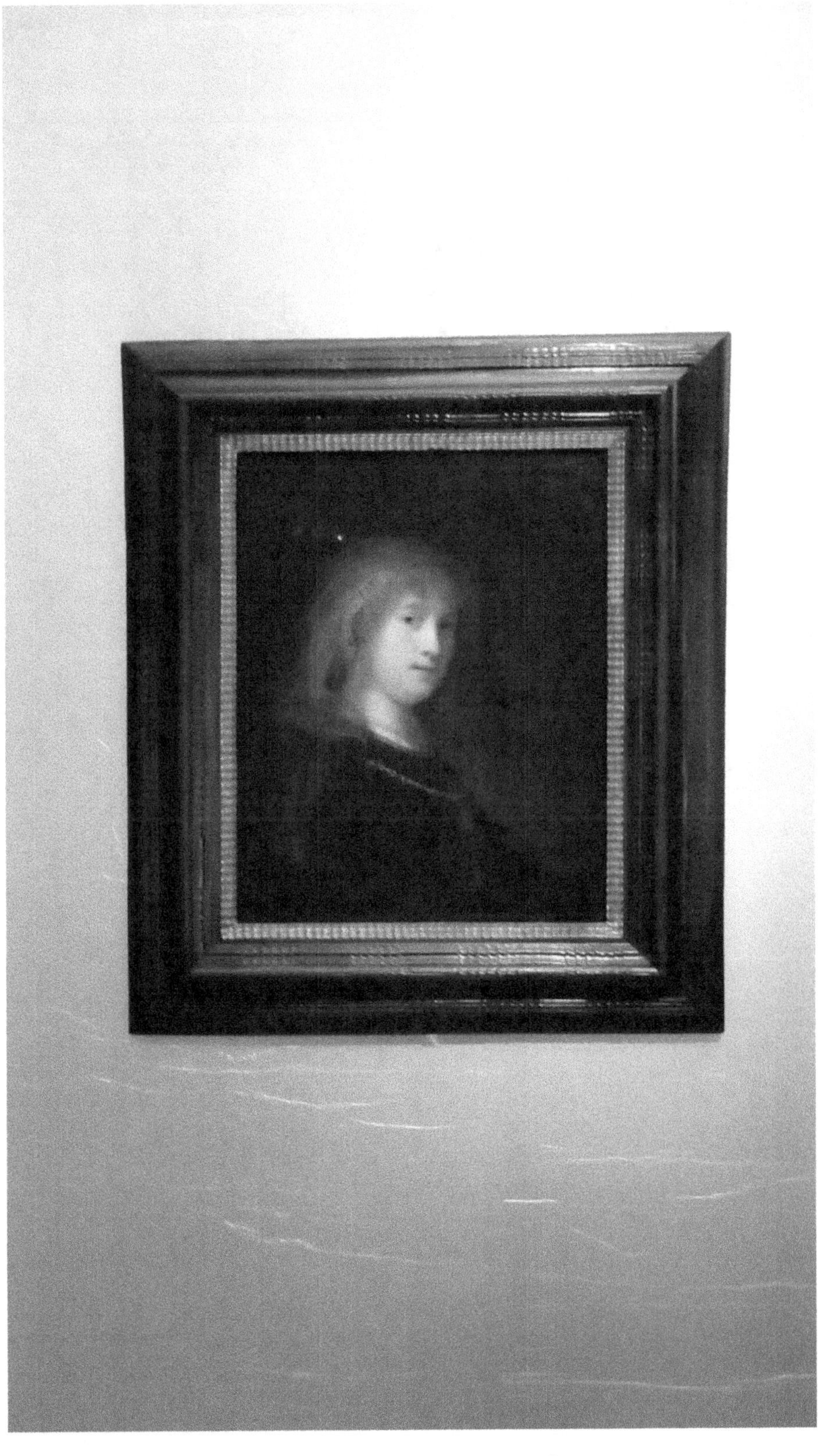

Rembrandt, Self-Portrait, Amsterdam

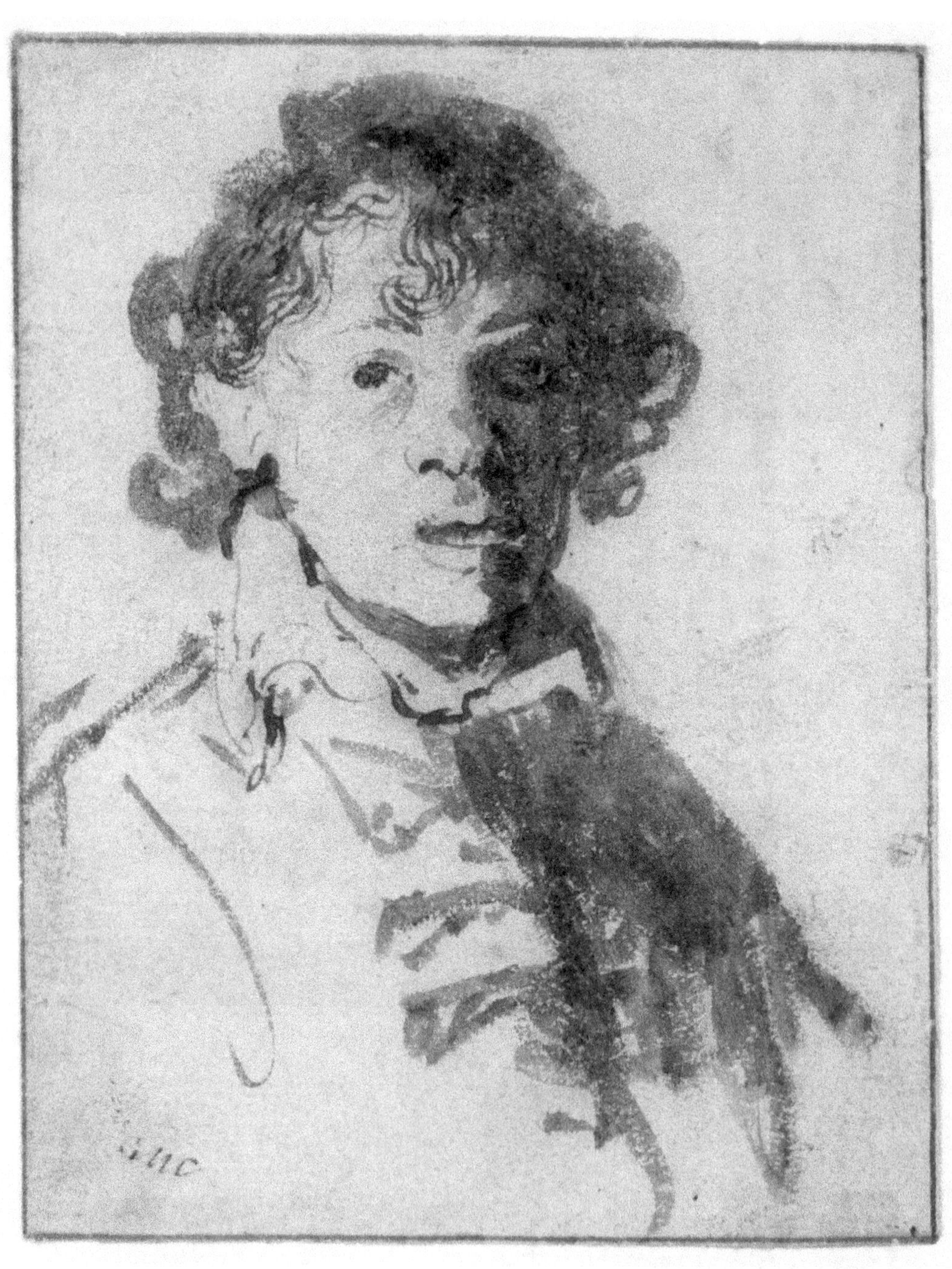

Rembrandt van Rijn, Self-Portrait With Open Mouth, 1629, British Museum

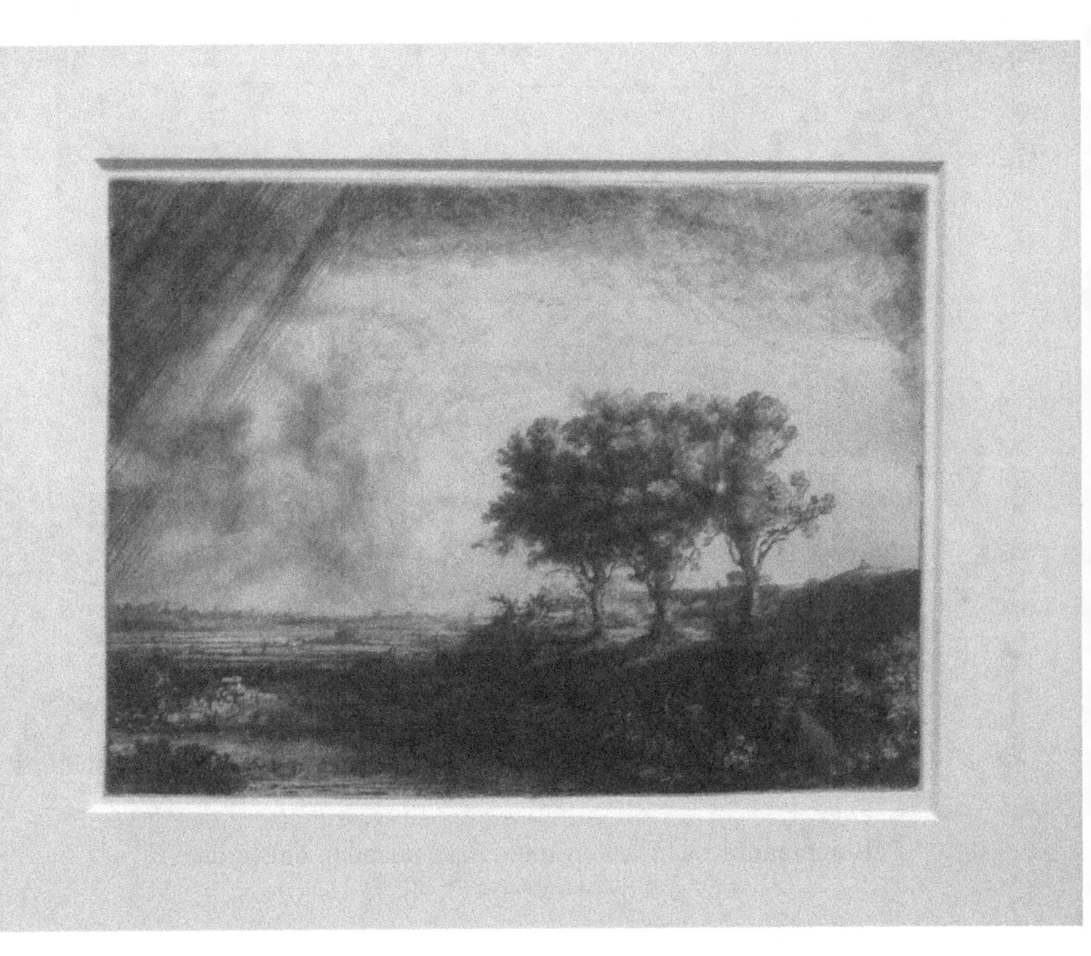

Rembrandt, Three Trees

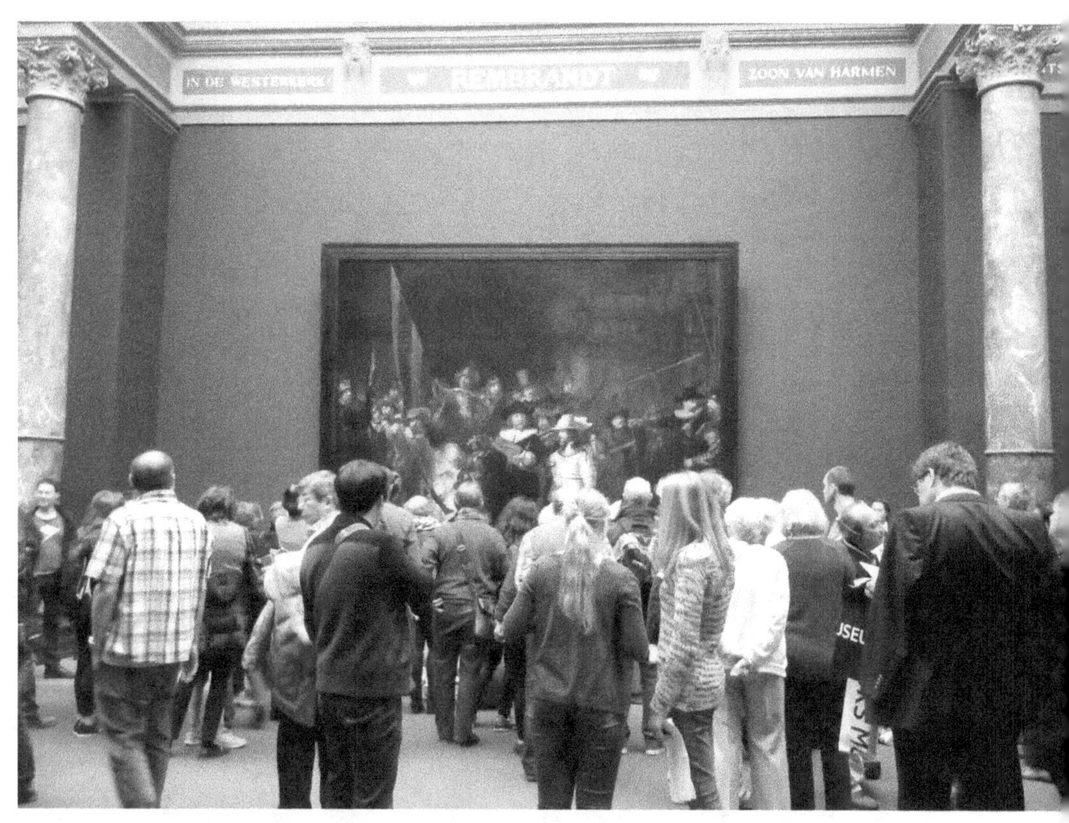

Rembrandt's Night Watch in the Rijksmuseum, Amsterdam
(photo: J. Robinson, 2015)

TO
THE EARL OF ELLESMERE,
THE ENLIGHTENED PATRON OF ART AND LITERATURE,
THIS WORK
IS MOST RESPECTFULLY INSCRIBED,

BY HIS OBLIGED, HUMBLE SERVANT,
JOHN BURNET.

PREFACE

The high estimation in which I have ever held the works of Rembrandt has been greatly increased by my going through this examination of his various excellencies, and such will ever be the case when the emanations of genius are investigated; like the lustre of precious stones, their luminous colour shines from the centre, not from the surface. With such a mine of rich ore as the works of Rembrandt contain, it is necessary to apologise for the paucity of examples offered, for in a work of this kind I have been obliged to confine myself to a certain brevity and a limited number of illustrations; still I must do my publisher the justice to say, he has not grudged any expense that would be the means of doing credit to the great artist, the enlightened patron, or my own reputation. Another circumstance has been elicited in preparing this work for publication – the great interest that all have shown in this humble attempt to make Rembrandt and his works more generally appreciated. His genius and productions seem to be congenial to the English taste. As a colourist he will ultimately lay the foundation of the British School of Painting, and prove the justice of Du Fresnoy's lines –

> "He who colours well must colour bright;
> Think not that praise to gain by sickly white."

Had it been possible, I would have given some examples of

his colour as well as of his chiaro-scuro; but I found his great charm consists more in the tone of his colouring than its arrangement. I have mentioned in the body of the work that Sir Joshua, certainly the greatest master of colour we have yet had in England, frequently speaks ambiguously of many of Rembrandt's pictures. I am therefore bound to quote a remark that he makes to his praise. In his Memoranda he says – "I considered myself as playing a great game; and instead of beginning to save money, I laid it out faster than I got it, in purchasing the best examples of art that could be procured, for I even borrowed money for this purpose. The possession of pictures by Titian, Vandyke, Rembrandt, &c., I considered as the best kind of wealth."

With these remarks I must now launch the result of my labours, having had constantly in mind that feeling which an advocate has in a good cause, not to expect, by all his exertions, to increase the reputation of his client, but an anxiety not to damage it by his weakness. Before concluding I must again revert to the interest that all my friends have taken in the success of this publication; and though it may appear invidious to particularise any, I cannot omit mention of that enthusiastic admirer of Rembrandt, my young friend Mr. E. W. Cooke; the Messrs. Smith, of Lisle-street, the connoisseurs and extensive dealers in his Etchings; Mr. Carpenter, the keeper of the prints in the British Museum; and, lastly, my young literary friend, Mr. Peter Cunningham, who has, from the beginning, entered heartily into the cause of "Rembrandt and his Works."

Brompton, November 4th, 1848.

REMBRANDT

In commencing an account of the life of Rembrandt Van Rhÿn and his works, I feel both a pleasure and a certain degree of confidence, as, from my first using a pencil, his pictures have been my delight and gratification, which have continued to increase through a long life of investigation. Though I cannot expect to enhance the high estimation in which Rembrandt is held by all persons competent to appreciate his extraordinary powers, nevertheless, the publication of the results of my study may tend to spread a knowledge of his principles and practice, which may be advantageous to similar branches in other schools; for, notwithstanding that his style is in the greatest degree original and peculiar to himself, yet it is founded upon those effects existing in nature which are to be discovered, more or less, in the works of all the great masters of colouring and chiaro-scuro. Of his early life little is known; for, unless cradled in the higher circles of society, the early lives of eminent men frequently remain shrouded in obscurity. The development of their genius alone draws attention to their history, which is generally progressive; hence a retrospective view is ambiguous. Little is known either of Rembrandt's birth or the place of his death; what is known has already been related, from Houbraken to Bryan, and from Bryan to Nieuwenhuys, and anecdotes have accumulated, for something new must be said. It is, however, fortunate that in searching into the source from which this extraordinary artist drew his knowledge, we have only to look into the great book of Nature, which existed at the time of Apelles and Raffaelle; and, notwithstanding the diversity of styles adopted by all succeeding painters, beauties and peculiarities are still left sufficient to establish the highest reputation for any one who has the genius to perceive them, and the industry to make them apparent. This was the cause of Rembrandt's captivating excellence; neither a combination of Coreggio and Titian, nor of Murillo and Velasquez, but as if all the great principles of chiaro-scuro and colour were steeped and harmonized in the softening shades of twilight; and this we perceive in nature, producing the most soothing and bewitching results. These digressions may, however, come more properly into notice when Rembrandt's principles of colour come under review.

Rembrandt Van Rhÿn, the subject of this memoir, was born in the year 1606, between Leydendorp and Koukerk, in the neighbourhood of Leyden, on the Rhÿn, but certainly not in a mill, as there is no habitable dwelling in the one now known as his father's. My excellent young friend, Mr. E. W. Cooke, whose works breathe the true spirit of the best of the Dutch school, in a letter upon this subject, says –

"My dear Sir,

"I send you another sketch of the mill; the picture, including the doorzigte, or view out of the window, I painted on the spot, and that picture is now in the possession of the King of Holland, having taken it back with me to show him. The mill was a magazine for powder during the Spanish invasion; it was soon after converted into a corn mill, and was in the possession of Hernan Geritz Van Rhÿn when his son Rembrandt was born; it is situated at Koukerk, on the old Rhÿn, near Leyden. I hope you will correct the vulgar error that Rembrandt was born in a mill. There are often dwelling houses attached to water-mills, such as we have in England; but in Holland, not such a structure as a water-mill, with water-power; the water-mills there are only *draining mills*, such as we have in Lincolnshire, Norfolk, &c. Surely the noise and movement of a windmill would ill accord with

the confinement of any lady, especially the mother of so glorious a
fellow as *Rembrandt*. For the honour of such association I hope you
will not omit my name in the work, for I painted three pictures of that
precious relic.

"Yours, &c.
"E. W. Cooke."

The mill now known as the one possessed by Rembrandt's
father is built of stone, with an inscription, and *"Rembrandt,"* in
gold letters, over the door. The one etched by his eminent son is a
wooden structure, which must have long since fallen into decay.
As they are both interesting, from association of ideas, I have
given etchings of them.

The mother of Rembrandt was Neeltje Willems Van
Zuitbroek, whose portrait he has etched. As he was an only child,
his parents were anxious to give him a good education, and
therefore sent him to the Latin school at Leyden, in order to bring
him up to the profession of the law; but, like our own inimitable
Shakspere, he picked up "small Latin and less Greek." Having
shown an early inclination for painting, they placed him under
the tuition of Jacob Van Zwaanenburg, a painter unmentioned by
any biographer; he afterwards entered the studio of Peter
Lastman, and finally received instruction from Jacob Pinas. The
two last had visited Rome, but, notwithstanding, could have
given little instruction to Rembrandt, as their works show no
proof of their having studied the Italian school to much purpose.
After receiving a knowledge of a few rules, such as they could
communicate, he returned home, and commenced painting from
nature, when he laid the foundation of a style in art
unapproached either before his time or since. In 1627 he is said,
by Houbraken, to have visited the Hague, when, by the price he
received for one of his pictures, he discovered his value as an
artist. The neighbourhood of the Rhine was now given up for the
city of Amsterdam, where he set up his easel in the year 1628,
under the patronage of the Burgomaster Six, and other wealthy

admirers of the fine arts.

Rembrandt's first works, like all the early works of eminent artists, were carefully finished; the work that raised him to the greatest notice, in the first instance, is Professor Tulpius giving an Anatomical Lecture on a dead Body,[1] and is dated 1632. Reynolds, in his Tour through Flanders, speaking of this picture, says: – "The Professor Tulpius dissecting a corpse which lies on the table, by Rembrandt. To avoid making it an object disagreeable to look at, the figure is just cut at the wrist. There are seven other portraits, coloured like nature itself; fresh, and highly finished. One of the figures behind has a paper in his hand, on which are written the names of the rest. Rembrandt has also added his own name, with the date 1632. The dead body is perfectly well drawn, (a little foreshortened,) and seems to have been just washed; nothing can be more truly the colour of dead flesh. The legs and feet, which are nearest the eye, are in shadow; the principal light, which is on the body, is by that means preserved of a compact form; all these figures are dressed in black." He further adds – "Above stairs is another Rembrandt, of the same kind of subject: Professor Nieman, standing by a dead body, which is so much foreshortened that the hands and feet almost touch each other; the dead man lies on his back, with his feet towards the spectator. There is something sublime in the character of the head, which reminds one of Michelangelo; the whole is finely painted, – the colouring much like Titian."

Simeon in the Temple, in the Museum of the Hague, painted in 1631, is in his first manner; as are The Salutation, in the

---

1 Mr. Nieuwenhuys, in a note in his Life of Rembrandt, mentions that the Directors of the Anatomical Theatre resolved to sell this picture by auction, for the purpose of augmenting the funds for supporting the widows of members, and in consequence the sale was announced for Monday the 4th of August, 1828. Since the year 1632, until this period, it had always remained in that establishment, as a gift from Professor N. Tulp, who presented it as a remembrance of himself and colleagues. Mr. N. had no sooner heard that the piece in question was to be sold, than he went to Amsterdam, with the intention of purchasing it; but, upon arriving, was informed that his Majesty, the King of the Netherlands, had opposed the sale, and given orders to the Minister for the Home Department to obtain it for the sum of 32,000 guldens, and caused it to be placed in the Museum at the Hague, where it remains. The picture is on canvas: height 64–? inches, width 83–? inches.

Gallery of the Marquis of Westminster, painted in 1640; and The Woman taken in Adultery, in the National Gallery, painted in 1644, all on panel, and finished with the care and minuteness of Gerhard Dow. His most successful career may be taken from 1630 to 1656. About the year 1645 he married Miss Saskia Van Uylenburg, by whom he had an only son, named Titus, the inheritor of the little wealth left after his father's embarrassments, but, though bred to the arts, inheriting little of his father's genius. In what part of Amsterdam he resided at this time we have no record, nor is the house now shown as Rembrandt's, and which was the subject of a mortgage, sufficiently authenticated to prove its identity; he may have lived in it, but it could not at any time have been sufficiently capacious to contain all the effects given in the catalogue extracted from the register by Mr. Nieuwenhuys.

The late Sir David Wilkie, in a letter to his sister, says: – "At the Hague we were delayed with rain, which continued nearly the whole of our way through Leyden, Haarlem, and Amsterdam. Wherever we went, our great subject of interest was seeing the native places of the great Dutch painters, and the models and materials which they have immortalized. At Amsterdam we sallied forth in the evening, in search of the house of Rembrandt; it is in what is now the Jews' quarter, and is, in short, a Jew's old china shop; it is well built, four stories high, but it greatly disappointed me. The shop is high in the ceiling, but all the other rooms are low and little, and, compared with the houses of Titian at Venice, of Claude at Rome, and of Rubens at Antwerp, is quite unworthy the house of the great master of the school of Holland. Even if stuffed, as it is now, with every description of the pottery of Canton, it could not have held even a sixth part of the inventory Nieuwenhuys found, as the distrained effects of Rembrandt, and the only solution is, that he may have once lived there; but as his will, still extant, is dated in another street, and as several of the pictures he painted could not be contained in the rooms we were in, we must conclude that, like the shell which encloses the caterpillar, it was only a temporary abode for the

☆ 22

winged genius to whom art owes so much of its brilliancy."

As the place of his residence is veiled in obscurity, so is the place of his demise, which is supposed to have taken place in 1664, as Mr. Smith, in a note to his Life of Rembrandt, says – "that no picture is recorded bearing a later date than 1664, and the balance of his property was paid over to his son in 1665."

Mr. Woodburn, in a Catalogue of his Drawings, says: – "It is uncertain what became of him after his bankruptcy, or where he died; a search has been made among the burials at Amsterdam, until the year 1674, but his name does not occur; probably Baldinucci is correct in stating that he died at Stockholm, in 1670;" others have mentioned Hull, and some give a credence to his having fled to Yarmouth, during his troubles, and mention two pictures, a lawyer and his wife, said to have been painted there; they are whole lengths, and certainly in his later manner, but I could not gather any authentic account to build conjecture upon, as the intercourse between Amsterdam and Yarmouth has been kept up from olden time, and a Dutch fair held every three years on the shore. The ancestors of the family in whose possession they still are, may have visited Holland; but, amongst such conflicting opinions, it is useless to attempt elucidation of the truth of this. We may rest certain that his works will be appreciated in proportion as a knowledge of their excellence is extended.

Extract from the Book of Sureties of Real Estates remaining at the Secretary's Office of the City of Amsterdam, fol. 89, &c.

Legal Receipt and Discharge, given by Titus Van Ryn, for the Balance of the Estate of his Father, Rembrandt Van Ryn.

Good for Gls. 6952–9.
the 29.7bre – Willem Muilm.

I the undersigned acknowledge to have received of the said Commissaries the undermentioned six thousand nine hundred and fifty-two Guldens nine Stuivers, the 5th November, 1665.

Received the contents, Titus Van Ryn.

Before the undersigned Magistrates appeared Titus Van Ryn, the only surviving son of Rembrandt Van Ryn and of Saskia Van Uylenburg (having obtained his veniam ætatis), as principal, – Abraham Fransz, merchant, living in the Angelier Straat, and Bartholomeus Van Benningen, woollen-draper, in the Liesdel, as guarantees. And jointly, and each of them separately, promised to re-deliver into the hands of the Commissaries of the Insolvent Estates, when called upon, the said six thousand nine hundred fifty-two Guldens and nine Stuivers, which the said Titus Van Ryn shall receive of and from the before-mentioned Commissaries, the money arising from the house and ground in the Anthonis bree Straat, A.° 1658, which was sold under execution, and from the personal estate of Saskia Van Uylenburg and Rembrandt Van Ryn aforesaid; hereby binding all their goods, moveables, and immoveables, present and future, in order to recover the said sum and costs. Therefore the before-mentioned principal promised to indemnify his said sureties under a similar obligation as above written. – Actum, the 9th September, 1665.

A. J. J. Hinlopen and Arnout Hooft.
H. V. Bronchorst.

2207 : a 3 : 3 6952 : 1
(Stamp)   8
____

6952   9

PICTURES, & c.

The following Catalogue is extracted from the Register L[a] R. fol. 29 to 39 inclusive, of the Inventory of the Effects of **Rembrandt Van Rhyn,** *deposited in the Office of the Administration of Insolvent Estates at Amsterdam, Anno 1656.*

IN THE ENTRANCE HALL.

A Picture, representing The Gingerbread Baker
By *Brauwer*.

A ditto, The Gamblers
Ditto.

A ditto, A Woman and Child
Rembrandt.

A ditto, The Interior of an Artist's Painting Room
Brauwer.

A ditto, The Interior of a Kitchen
Ditto.

A Statue of a Woman, in plaster.

Two Children, in plaster.

A Sleeping Child, in plaster.

A Landscape
By *Rembrandt*.

A ditto
Ditto.

A Woman represented standing
Ditto.

A Christmas Night Piece
Jean Lievensz.

St. Jerome
Rembrandt.

Dead Hares, a small picture
Ditto.

A small picture of a Pig
Ditto.

A small Landscape
Hercules Segers.

A Landscape
Jean Lievensz.

A ditto
Ditto.

A ditto
Rembrandt.

A Combat of Lions
Ditto.

A Landscape, by moonlight
Jean Lievensz.

A Head
Rembrandt.

A ditto
Ditto.

A picture of Still Life, objects retouched
Ditto.

A Soldier, clad in armour
By *Rembrandt.*

A Skull, and other objects, styled a Vanitas, retouched
Ditto.

A ditto, ditto, retouched
Ditto.

A Sea Piece
Hendrick Antonisz.

Four Spanish Chairs, covered with leather.

Two ditto, ditto in black.

A Plank of Wood.

IN THE FRONT PARLOUR.

A small picture of the Samaritan, retouched
By *Rembrandt*.

The Rich Man
Palma Vecchio.
(The half of this picture belongs to *Peter de la Tombe*).

A View of the Back of a House
By *Rembrandt*.

Two Sporting Dogs, done after nature
Ditto.

The Descent from the Cross, a large picture, in a gilt frame
Ditto.

The Raising of Lazarus
Ditto.

A Courtesan Dressing
Ditto.

A Woody Scene
Hercules Segers.

Tobias, &c.
Lastman.

The Raising of Lazarus
Jean Lievensz.

A Landscape, representing a mountainous country
Rembrandt.

A small Landscape
By *Govert Jansz.*

Two Heads
Rembrandt.

A Picture, *en grisaille*
Jean Lievensz.

A ditto, *ditto*
Parcelles.

A Head
Rembrandt.

A ditto
Brauwer.

A View of the Dutch Coast
Parcelles.

A ditto of the same, smaller
Ditto.

A Hermit
Jean Lievensz.

Two Small Heads
Lucas Van Valkenburg.

A Camp on Fire

The elder Rassan.

A Quack Doctor
After Brauwer.

Two Heads
By *Jan Pinas.*

A perspective View
Lucas Van Leyden.

A Priest
Jean Lievensz.

A Model
Rembrandt.

A Flock of Sheep
Ditto.

A Drawing
Ditto.

The Flagellation of our Lord
Ditto.

A Picture, done *en grisaille*
Parcelles.

A ditto, ditto
Simon de Vlieger.

A small Landscape
Rembrandt.

A Head of a Woman, after Nature
Ditto.

A Head
Rafaelle Urbino.

A View of Buildings, after Nature
Rembrandt.

A Landscape, after Nature
Ditto.

A View of Buildings
Hercules Segers.

The Goddess Juno
Jacob Pinas.

A Looking Glass, in a black ebony frame.

An ebony Frame.

A Wine Cooler, in marble.

A Table of walnut tree, covered with a carpet.

Seven Spanish Chairs, with green velvet cushion.

BACK PARLOUR.

A Picture
By *Pietro Testa.*

A Woman with a Child

Rembrandt.

Christ on the Cross, a model
Ditto.

A Naked Woman
Ditto.

A Copy, after a picture
Annibal Caracci.

Two Half Figures
Brauwer.

A Copy, after a picture
Annibal Caracci.

A Sea View
Parcelles.

The Head of an Old Woman
Van Dyck.

A Portrait of a deceased Person
Abraham Vink.

The Resurrection
A. Van Leyden.

A Sketch
Rembrandt.

Two Heads, after Nature
Ditto.

The Consecration of Solomon's Temple, done *en grisaille*
Ditto.

The Circumcision, a copy
After *Ditto*.

Two small Landscapes
By *Hercules Segers*.

A gilt Frame.

A small Oak Table.

Four Shades for engraving.

A Clothes Press.

Four old Chairs.

Four green Chair Cushions.

A Copper Kettle.

A Portmanteau.

THE SALOON.

A Woody Scene
By *An Unknown Master*.

An Old Man's Head
Rembrandt.

A large Landscape

Hercules Segers.

A Portrait of a Woman
Rembrandt.

An Allegory of the Union of the Country
Ditto.

This is probably the picture now in the Collection of Samuel Rogers, Esq.

A View in a Village
By *Govert Jansz.*

A Young Ox, after Nature
Rembrandt.

The Samaritan Woman, a large picture, attributed to *Giorgione,* the half of which belongs to *Peter de la Tombe.*

Three antique Statues.

A Sketch of the Entombment
By *Rembrandt.*

The Incredulity of St. Peter
Aertje Van Leyden.

The Resurrection of our Lord
Rembrandt.

The Virgin Mary
Rafaelle Urbino.

A Head of Christ

Rembrandt.

A Winter Scene
Grimaer.

The Crucifixion. Probably intended for *Novellari
Lely of Novellaene.*

A Head of Christ
Rembrandt.

A young Bull or Ox
Lastman.

A Vanitas, retouched
Rembrandt.

An Ecce Homo, *en grisaille*
Ditto.

Abraham Offering up his Son
Jean Lievensz.

A Vanitas, retouched
Rembrandt.

A Landscape, *en grisaille*
Hercules Segers.

An Evening Scene
Rembrandt.

A large Looking Glass.

Six Chairs, with blue cushions.

An oak Table.

A Table Cloth.

A Napkin Press.

A Wardrobe, or Armoir.

A Bed and a Bolster.

Two Pillows.

Two Coverlids.

Blue Hangings of a Bed.

A Chair.

A Stove.

IN THE CABINET OF ARTS.

A pair of Globes.

A Box, containing minerals.

A small Architectural Column.

A Tin Pot.

The Figure of an Infant.

Two pieces of Indian Jadd.

A Japan or Chinese Cup.

A Bust of an Empress.

An Indian Powder Box.

A Bust of the Emperor Augustus.

An Indian Cup.

A Bust of the Emperor Tiberius.

An Indian Work-Box, for a lady.

A Bust of Caius.

A pair of Roman Leggins.

Two Porcelain Figures.

A Bust of Heraclitus.

Two Porcelain Figures.

A Bust of Nero.

Two Iron Helmets.

An Indian Helmet.

An ancient Helmet.

A Bust of a Roman Emperor.

A Negro, cast from Nature.

A Bust of Socrates.

A Bust of Homer.

A ditto of Aristotle.

An antique Head, done in brown.

A Faustina.

A Coat of Armour, and a Helmet.

A Bust of the Emperor Galba.

A ditto of the Emperor Otho.

A ditto of the Emperor Vitellius.

A ditto of the Emperor Vespasian.

A ditto of the Emperor Titus Vespasian.

A ditto of the Emperor Domitian.

A ditto of Silius Brutus.

Forty-seven specimens of Botany.

Twenty-three ditto of Land and Marine Animals.

A Hammock, and two Calabashes.

Eight various objects, in plaster, done from Nature.

ON THE LAST SHELF.

A quantity of Shells, Marine Plants, and sundry curious objects, in plaster, done from Nature.

An antique Statue of Cupid.

A small Fuzil, and a Pistol.

A steel Shield, richly embossed with Figures, by Quintin Matsys, very curious and rare.

An antique Powder-horn.

A ditto; Turkish.

A Box, containing Medals.

A Shield of curious workmanship.

Two Naked Figures.

A Cast from the face of Prince Maurice, taken after his death.

A Lion and a Bull, in plaster, after Nature.

A number of Walking Sticks.

A long Bow.

BOOKS ON ART.

A Book, containing Sketches by *Rembrandt*.

A ditto, containing Prints engraved in wood by *Lucas Van Leyden*.

A ditto ditto, by *Wael and others*.

A ditto, containing Etchings by *Baroccio and Vanni*.

A ditto, containing Prints after *Rafaelle Urbino*.

A gilt Model of a French Bed, by *Verhulst*.

A Book full of Engravings, many of which are double impressions, by *Lucas Van Leyden*.

A ditto, containing a great number of Drawings by the best masters.

A ditto, containing a number of fine Drawings by *Andrea Mantegna*.

A ditto, containing Drawings by various masters, and some Prints.

A ditto, larger, full of Drawings and Prints.
A ditto, containing a number of Miniatures, Wood-cuts, and Copper-plate Prints, of the various costumes of countries.

A Book, full of Prints by *Old Breughel*.

A ditto, containing Prints after *Rafaelle Urbino*.

A ditto, containing valuable Prints, after the same.

A ditto, full of Prints by *Tempesta*.

A ditto, containing Wood-cuts and Engravings by *Lucas Cranach*.

A ditto, containing Prints after the *Caracci* and *Guido*, and *Spagnoletti*.

A ditto, containing Engravings and Etchings by *Tempesta*.

A large Folio of ditto ditto, by *Ditto*.

A ditto ditto, various.

A Book, containing Prints by *Goltius* and *Müller*.

A ditto, containing Prints after *Rafaelle Urbino*, very fine impressions.

A Book, containing Drawings by *Brauwer*.

A Folio, containing a great number of Prints after *Titian*.

A number of curious Jars and Venetian Glasses.

An old Book, containing a number of Sketches by *Rembrandt*.

A ditto ditto.

A large Folio of Sketches by *Rembrandt*.

An empty Folio.

A Backgammon Board.

An antique Chair.

A Book, containing Chinese Drawings in miniature.

A large Cluster of White Coral.

A Book full of Prints of Statues.

A ditto full of Prints, a complete work by *Heemskirk*.

A ditto, full of Sketches by *Rubens*, *Van Dyck*, and other masters.

A ditto, containing the Works of *Michelangelo Buonarotti*.

Two small Baskets.

A Book, containing Prints of free Subjects, after *Rafaelle*, *Roest*, *Annibal Caracci*, and *Giulio Romano*.

A ditto, full of Landscapes by the most distinguished masters.

A Book, containing Views of Buildings in Turkey, by *Melchoir Lowick*, *Hendrick Van Helst*, and others; and also the Costumes of that Country.

An Indian Basket, containing various Engravings by *Rembrandt*, *Hollar*, *Cocq*, and others.

A Book, bound in black leather, containing a selection of Etchings by *Rembrandt*.

A paper Box, full of Prints by *Hupe Martin*, *Holbein*, *Hans Broemer*, and *Israel Mentz*.

A Book, containing a complete set of Etchings by *Rembrandt*.

A Folio, containing Academical Drawings of Men and Women, by *Rembrandt*.

A Book, containing Drawings of celebrated Buildings in Rome, and other Views, by the best masters.

A Chinese Basket, full of various Ornaments.

A Folio.

A ditto.

A ditto, containing Landscapes after Nature by *Rembrandt*.

A Book, containing a selection of Proof Prints after *Rubens* and *Jacques Jordaens*.

A ditto, full of Drawings by *Miervelt*, *Titian*, and others.

A Chinese Basket.

A ditto ditto, containing Prints of Architectural Subjects.

A ditto, containing Drawings of various Animals from Nature by *Rembrandt*.

A ditto, full of Prints after *Frans Floris*, *Bruitwael*, *Goltius*, and *Abraham Bloemart*.

A quantity of Drawings from the Antique, by *Rembrandt*.

Five Books, in quarto, containing Drawings by *Rembrandt*.

A Book full of Prints of Architectural Views.

The Medea, a Tragedy, by *Jan Six*.

A quantity of Prints, by *Jacques Callot*.
A Book, bound in parchment, containing Drawings of Landscapes, after Nature, by *Rembrandt*.

A ditto, full of Sketches of Figures by *Rembrandt*.

A ditto, various.

A small Box, with wood divisions.

A Book, containing Views drawn by *Rembrandt*.

A ditto, containing fine Sketches.

A ditto, containing Statues after Nature by *Rembrandt*.

A ditto, various.

A ditto, containing pen Sketches by *Peter Lastman*.

A ditto, containing Drawings in red chalk by *Ditto*.

A ditto, containing Sketches drawn with the pen by *Rembrandt*.

A ditto, various.

A ditto, ditto.

A Book, various.

A ditto, ditto.

A ditto, ditto.

A Folio of large Drawings of Views in the Tyrol, by *Roeland Savery*.

A ditto, full of Drawings by celebrated masters.

A Book, in quarto, containing Sketches by *Rembrandt*.

A Book of Wood-cuts of the proportions of the Human Figure, by *Albert Durer*.

A Book, containing Engravings by *Jean Lievensz* and *Ferdinand Bol*.

Several parcels of Sketches by *Rembrandt* and others.

A quantity of Paper, of a large size.

A Box, containing Prints by *Van Vliet*, after Pictures by *Rembrandt*.

A Screen, covered with cloth.

A steel Gorget.

A Drawer, containing a Bird of Paradise, and six Forms of divers patterns.

A German Book, containing Prints of Warriors.

A ditto, with Wood-cuts.

Flavius Josephus, in German, illustrated with Engravings by *Tobias Kinderman*.

An ancient Bible.

A marble Inkstand.

A Cast, in Plaster, of Prince Maurice.

IN AN ANTI-CHAMBER OF THE ROOM OF ARTS.

St. Joseph
By *Aertje Van Leyden*.

Three Prints, in frames.

The Salutation.

A Landscape after Nature
Rembrandt.

A Landscape
Hercules Segers.

The Descent from the Cross
Rembrandt.

A Head after Nature.

A Skull
Retouched by *Rembrandt*.

A Model, in plaster, of the Bath of Diana
By *Adam Van Vianen*.

A Model from Nature
Rembrandt.

A Picture of Three Puppies, after Nature
Titus Van Ryn.

A ditto of a Book
Ditto.

A Head of the Virgin

Ditto.

The Flagellation
A Copy after *Rembrandt.*

A Landscape by Moonlight
Retouched by *Ditto.*

A Naked Woman, a Model from Nature
By *Ditto.*

An unfinished Landscape from Nature
Ditto.

A Horse painted from Nature
By *Rembrandt.*

A small Picture
Young Hals.

A Fish, after Nature.

A Model, in plaster, of a Bason, adorned with Figures, by *Adam Van Vianen.*

An old Chest.

Four Chairs, with black leather seats.

A Table.

IN THE SMALL PAINTING ROOM.

Thirty-three pieces of Armour and Musical Instruments.

Sixty pieces of Indian Armour, and several Bows, Arrows, and Darts.

Thirteen bamboo Pipes, and several Flutes.

Thirteen objects, consisting of Bows, Arrows, Shields, &c.

A number of Heads and Hands, moulded from Nature, together with a Harp, and a Turkish Bow.

Seventeen Hands and Arms, moulded from Nature.

Some Stag Horns.

Five ancient Casques.

Four long Bows, and cross Bows.

Nine Gourds and Bottles.

Two modelled Busts of Bartholt Been and his Wife.

A plaster Cast from a Grecian Antique.

A Bust of the Emperor Agrippa.

A ditto of the Emperor Aurelius.

A Head of Christ, of the size of Life.

A Head of a Satyr.

A Sibil – Antique.

The Laocoon – Ditto.

A large Marine Vegetable.

A Vitellius.

A Seneca.

Three or four antique Heads of Women.

A metal Cannon.

A quantity of Fragments of antique Dresses, of divers colours.

Seven Musical stringed Instruments.

Two small Pictures by *Rembrandt*.

IN THE LARGE PAINTING ROOM.

Twenty Objects, consisting of Halberds and Swords of various kinds.

Dresses of an Indian Man and Woman.

Five Cuirasses.

A wooden Trumpet.

A Picture of Two Negroes by *Rembrandt*.

A Child by *Michelangelo Buonarotti*.

IN THE SHED.

The Skins of a Lion and a Lioness, and two Birds.

A large Piece, representing Diana.

A Bittern, done from Nature, by *Rembrandt*.

IN A SMALL ROOM.

Ten Paintings, of various sizes, by *Rembrandt*.

A Bed.

IN THE KITCHEN.

A pewter Pot.

Several Pots and Pans.

A small Table.

A Cupboard.

Several old Chairs.

Two Chair Cushions.

IN THE PASSAGE.

Nine Plates.

Two earthen Dishes.

THE LINEN (THEN AT THE WASHER-WOMAN'S).

Three Shirts.

Six Pocket Handkerchiefs.

Twelve Napkins.

Three Table Cloths.

Some Collars and Wristbands.

The preceding Inventory was made on the 25th and 26th of July, 1656.

Free Translation of the Autograph Letter on the opposite page.

Sir,

It is, your Honour, with reluctance, that I am about to trouble you
with a letter, and that, because on applying to the receiver
Utenbogaert, (to whom I have entrusted the management of my
money matters,) as to how the treasurer Volberger acquits himself of
the yearly 4 per cent. interest, the said Utenbogaert, on Wednesday
last, replied, – that Volberger has every half year received the interest
on this annuity, and has done so up to the present time; so that now, at
the annuity office, more than 4000 florins being owing, and this being
the exact and true statement, I beg of you, my kind-natured Sir, that
the exact sum of money at my disposal may be at once made clear, in
order that I may at last receive the sum of 1244 florins, long since due;
as I shall always strive to recompense such by reciprocal services,
and with lasting friendship; so that with my most cordial greetings,
and the prayer that God may long keep you in good health, and grant
you bliss hereafter,

    I remain,
    Your Honour's
    Obedient and devoted Servant,

REMBRANDT.

I am living on the Binnen Aemstel, at the Confectioner's.
10th Oct.

    Van Suylyken, Esq.
     Counsellor and Secretary to his Highness in the Hague.

Per post.

We cannot reflect upon the foregoing Catalogue without regretting that Rembrandt, in his old age, should have, like our own Milton,

"Fall'n on evil days,
On evil days though fall'n and evil tongues."

The troubles existing at that time pervaded the whole of Europe, and works, both of poetry and painting, produced little emolument to the possessors; consequently the whole of this rich assemblage of works of art, the accumulation of years, fell a sacrifice to the hammer of the auctioneer, producing little more than four thousand nine hundred guilders. By its list, however, we are enabled to refute the assertion of many of his biographers, that he neglected the antique, and the works of the great masters of the Italian school, the catalogue including casts from ancient sculpture, and drawings and prints after Michelangelo, Raffaelle, and Titian, which at that time were rare and of great value. We find by a memorandum on the back of one of Rembrandt's proofs, on India paper, of his etching of "Christ Healing the Sick," which now goes by the name of "The Hundred Guilder Print," that, "wishing to possess a print of the Plague, by Mark Antonio, after Raffaelle, valued by the dealer Van Zomers at a hundred florins, he gave the proof in exchange;" and further, "that such proofs were never sold, but given as presents to his friends." We may perceive by this the anxiety he had to collect works that were excellent. As we do not discover amongst the various articles enumerated, either palette or brushes, we may infer that on quitting Amsterdam he carried off all his working apparatus.

With this short notice of his life, and these few remarks, I must now enter into what is more properly the subject of this work, a critical examination into his principles and practice.

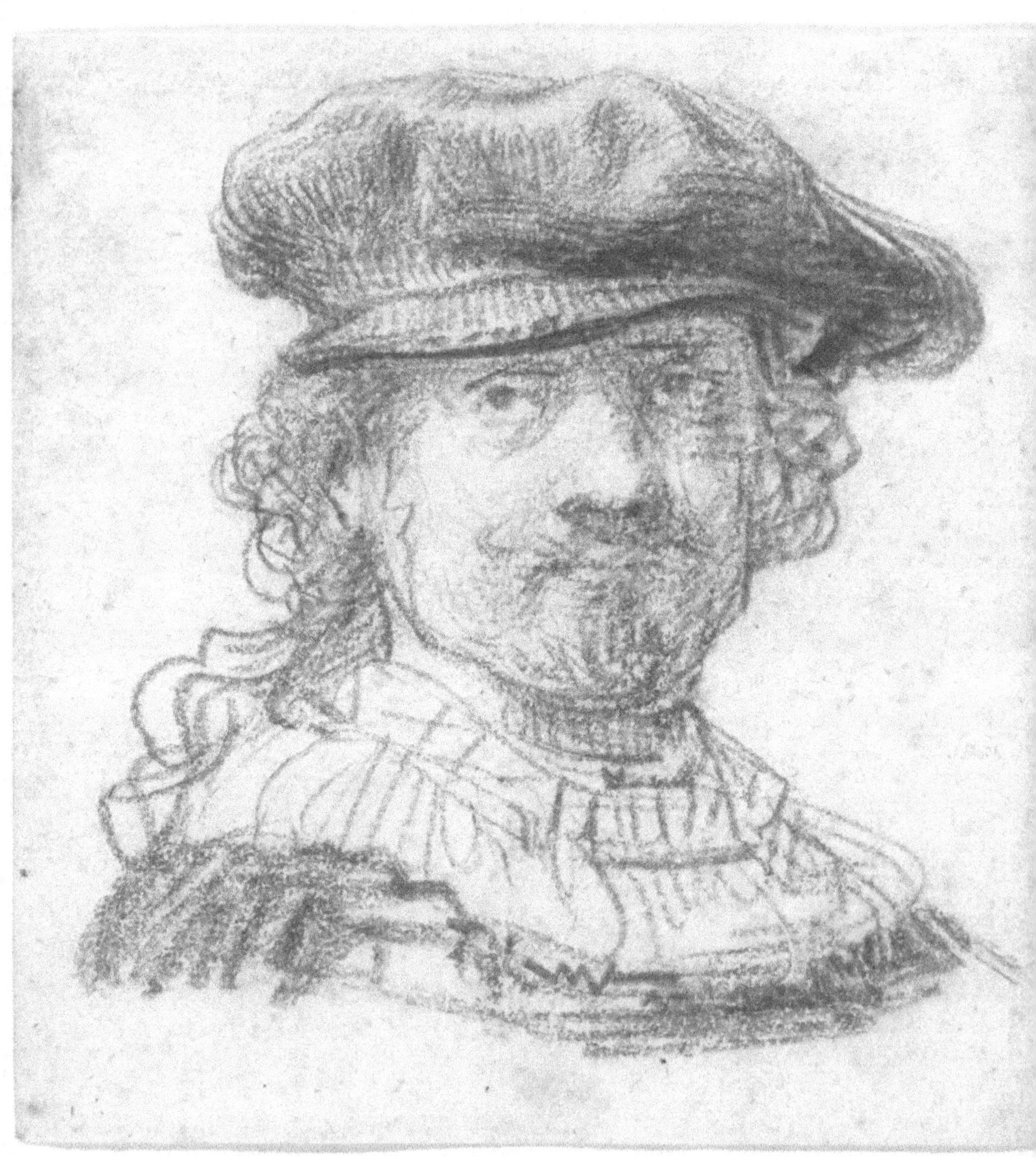

Rembrandt van Rijn, Self-Portrait, c.1637, Washington, DC

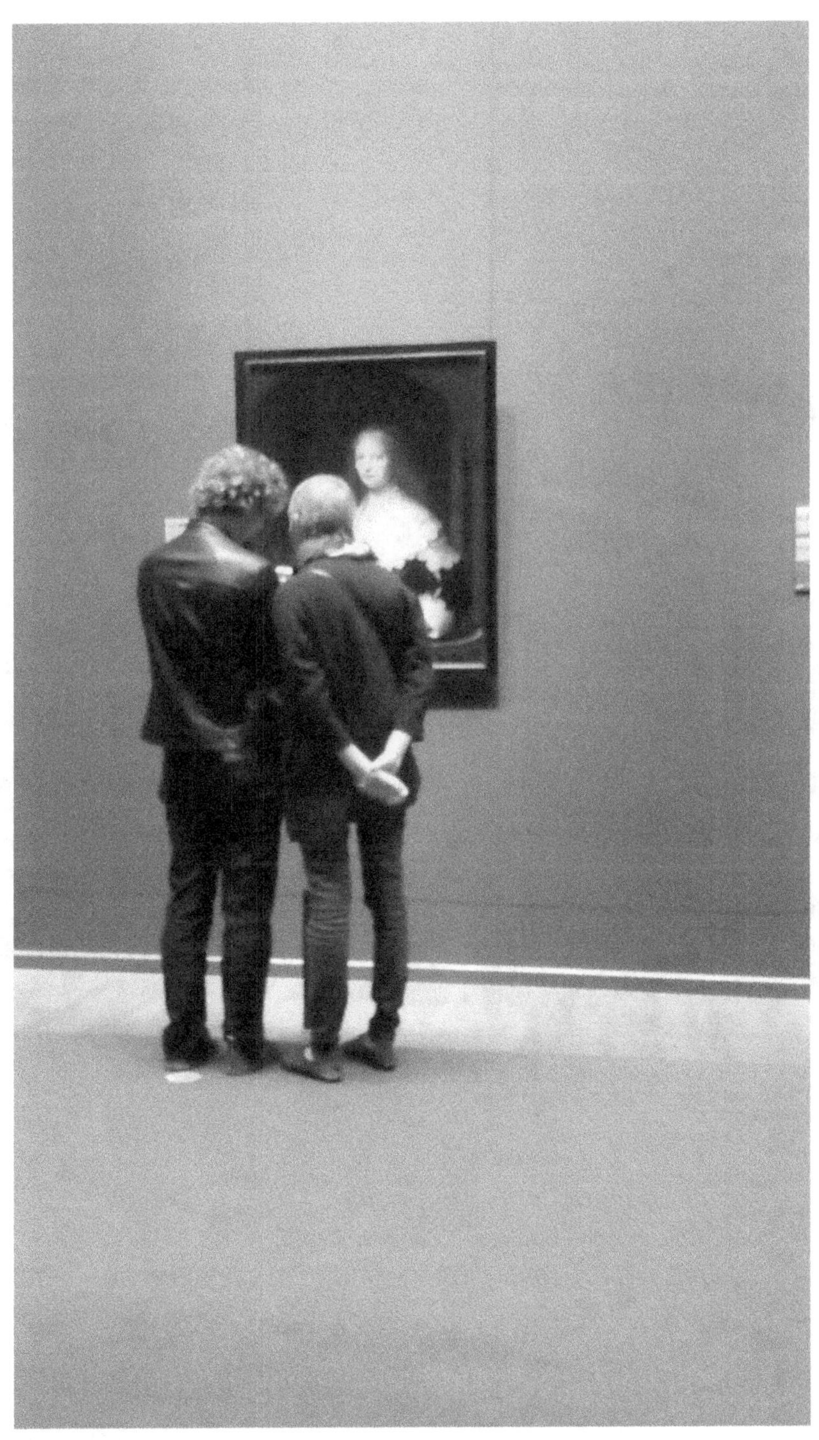

Rembrandt in the Rijksmusem, Amsterdam, 2015
(this page and over. Photos: J. Robinson).

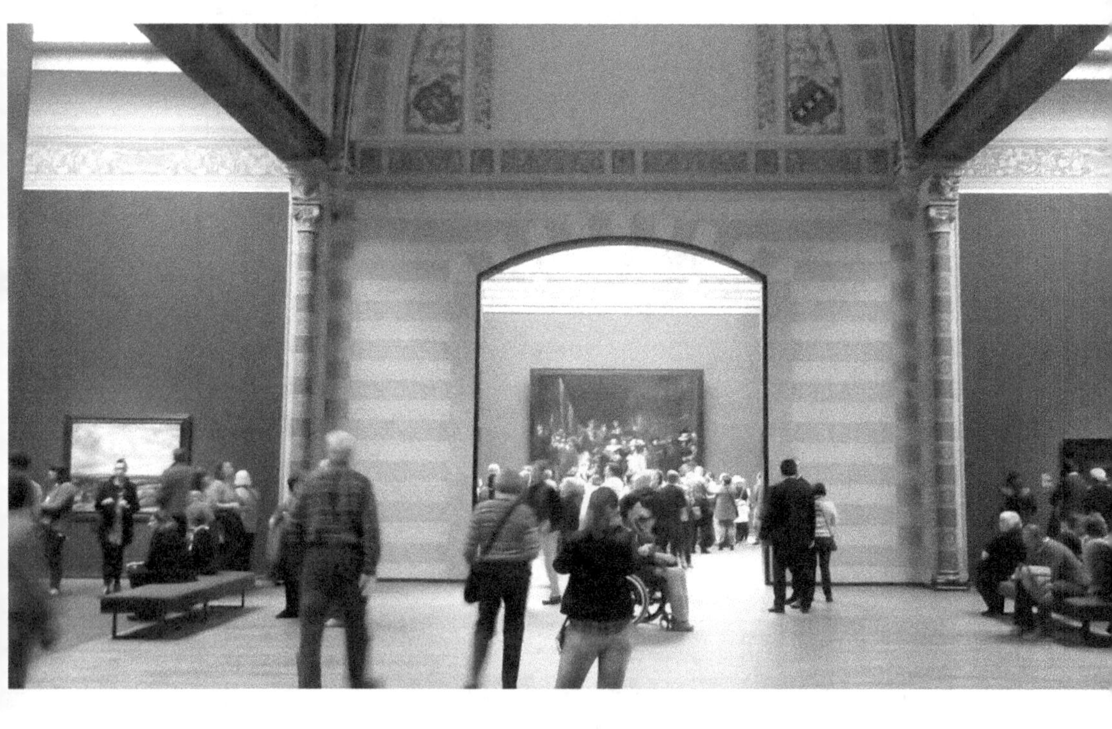

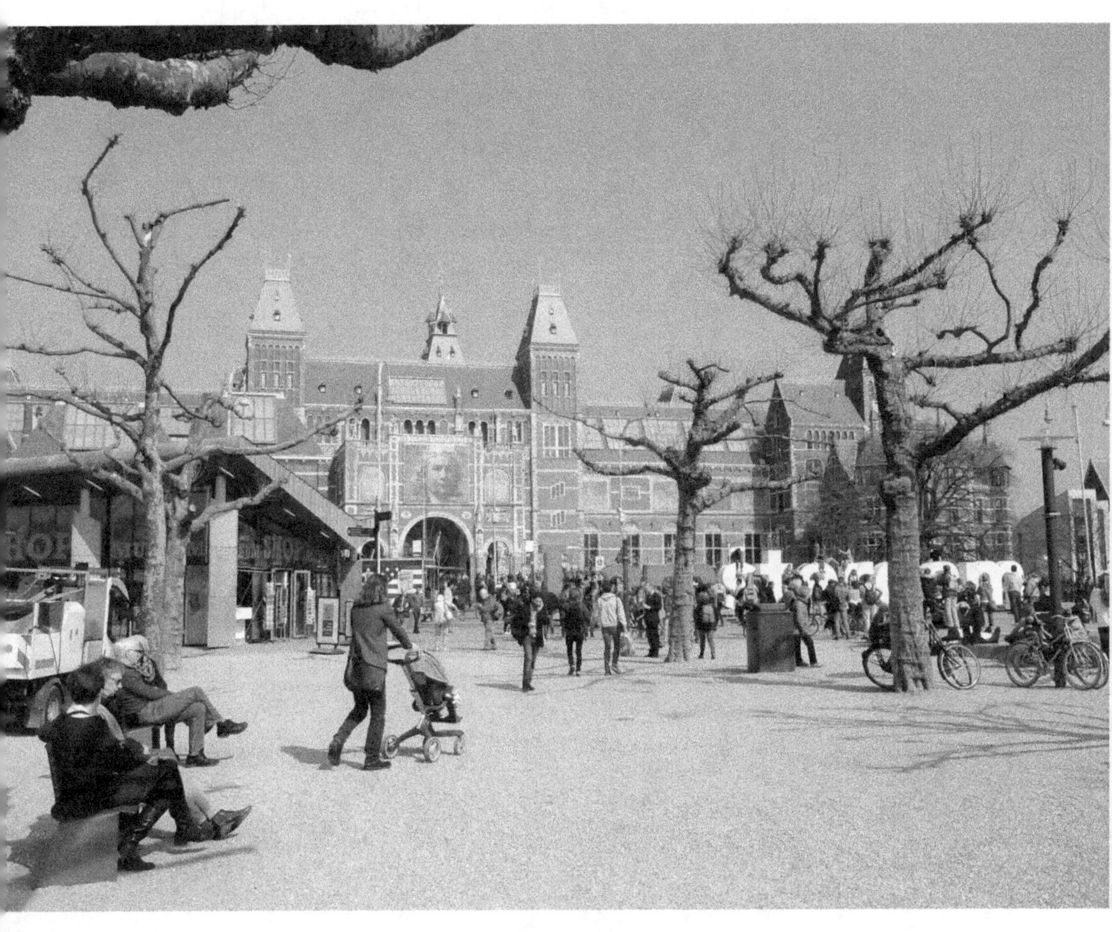

The Rijksmuseum in Amsterdam

Rembrandt, Self-Portrait, 1640, London
(this page and over)

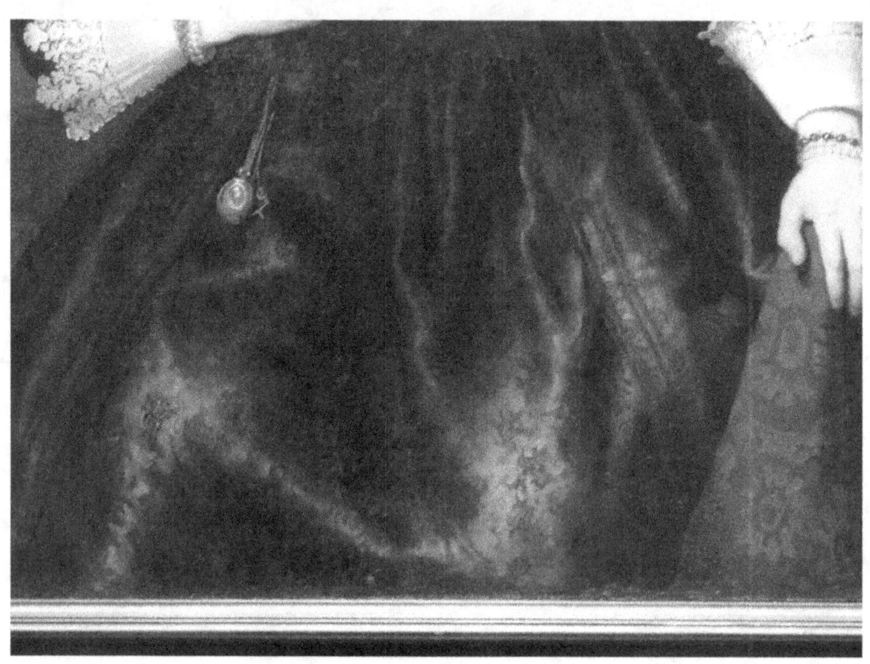

Rembrandt, Portrait of a Young Woman, details

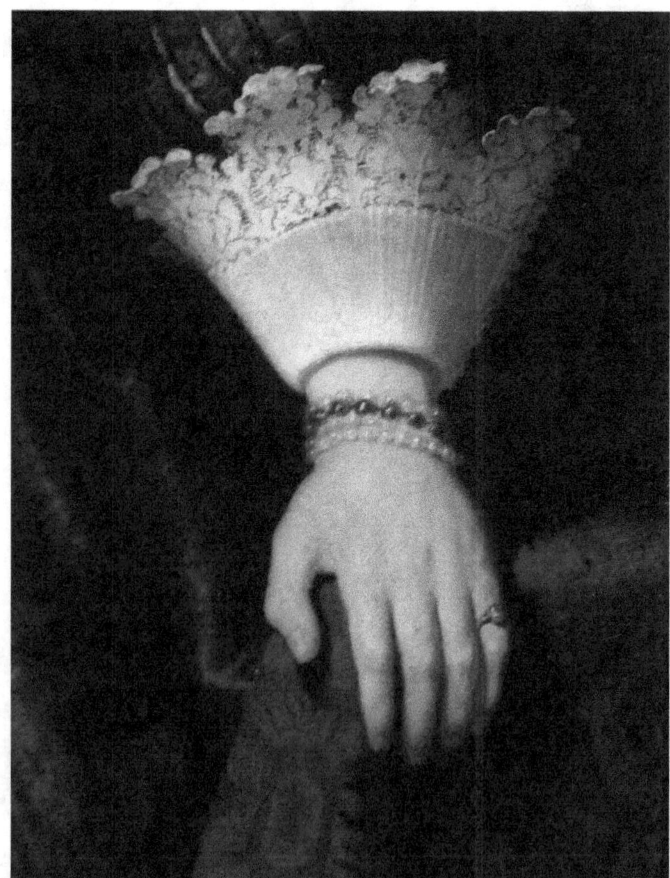

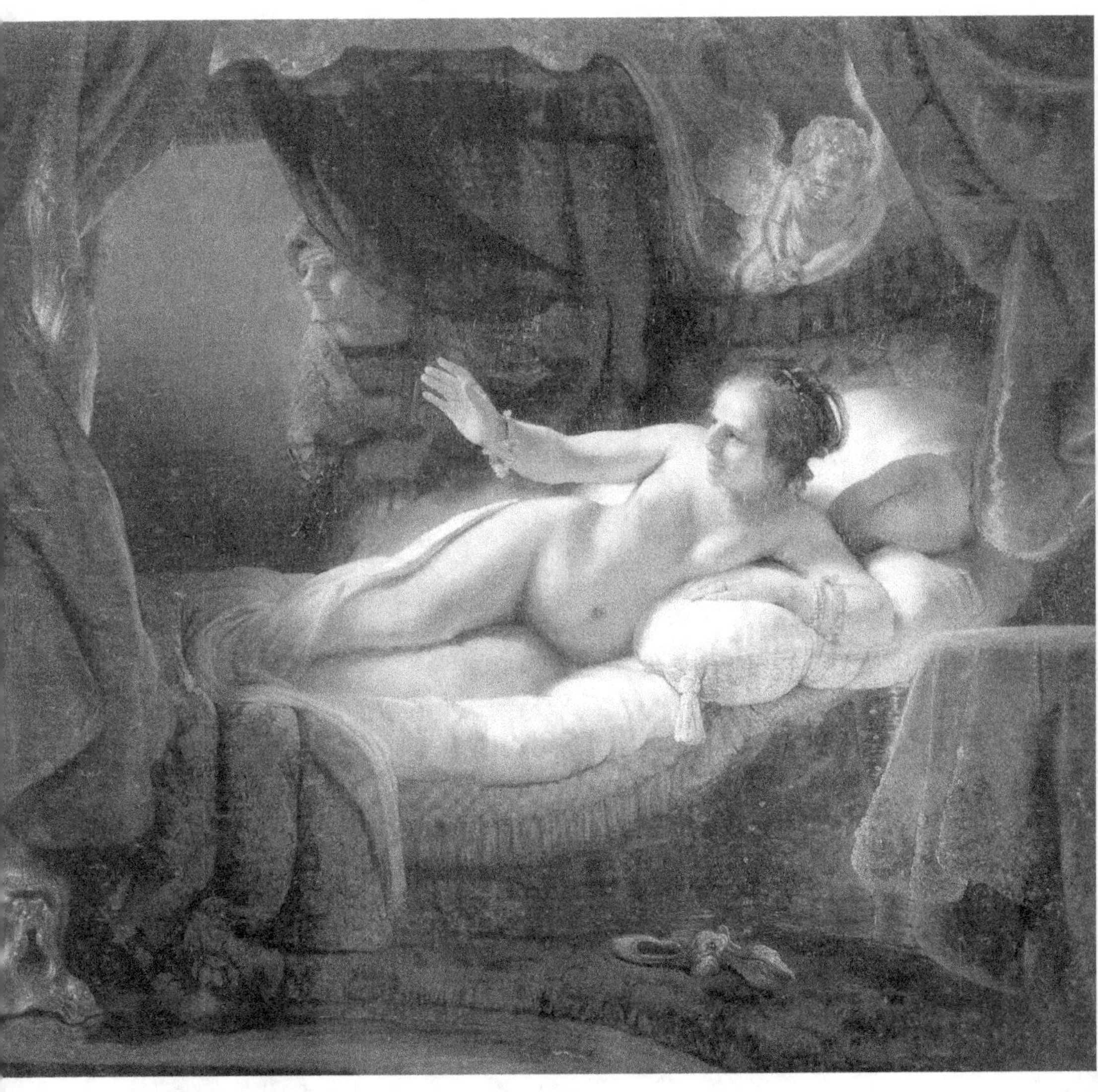

Rembrandt van Rijn, Danae, 1636, St Petersburg

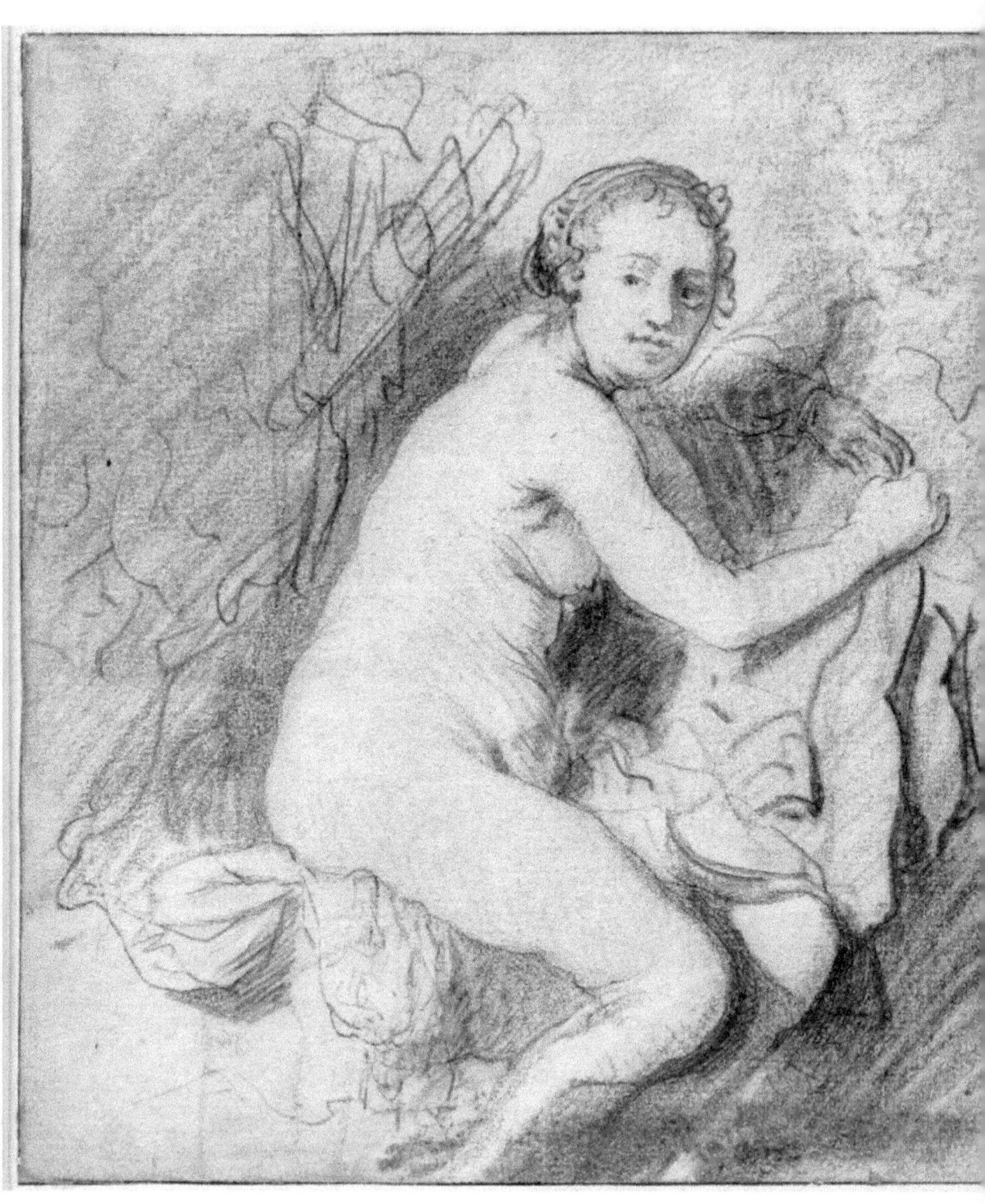

Rembrandt van Rijn, Diana At the Bath, 1630-31, British Museum

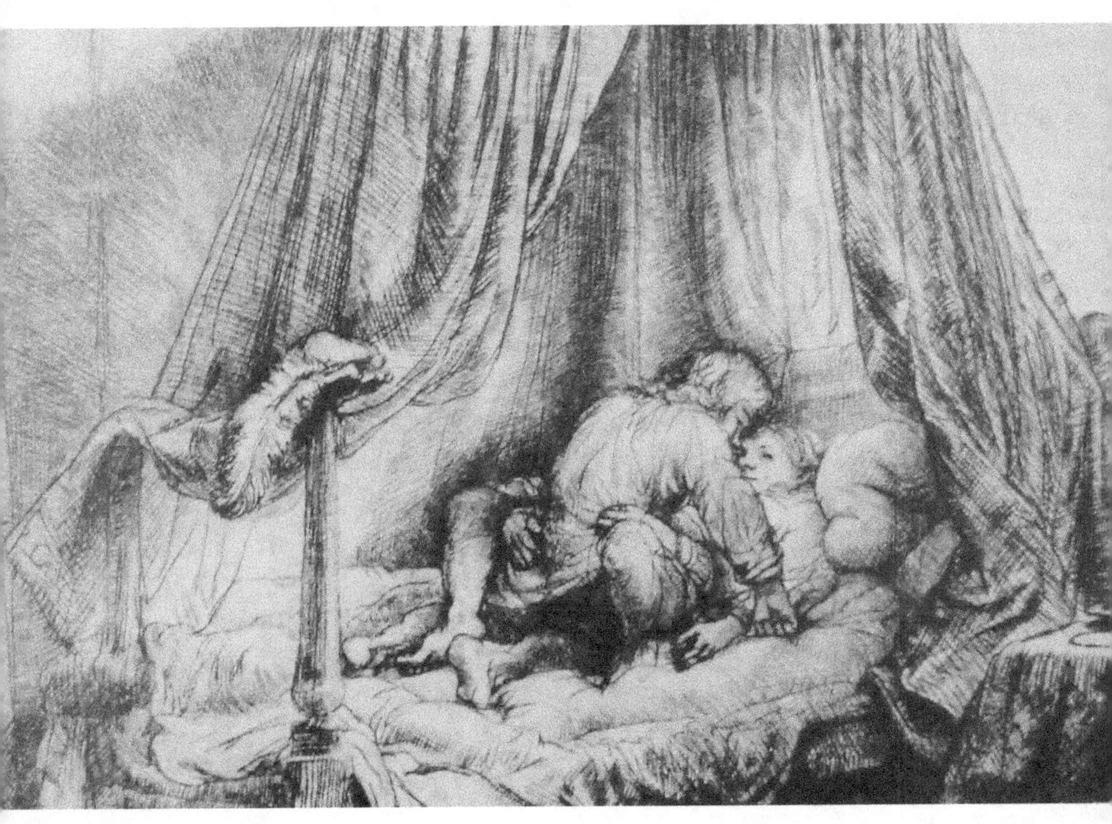

Rembrandt van Rijn, Ledakant, 1646

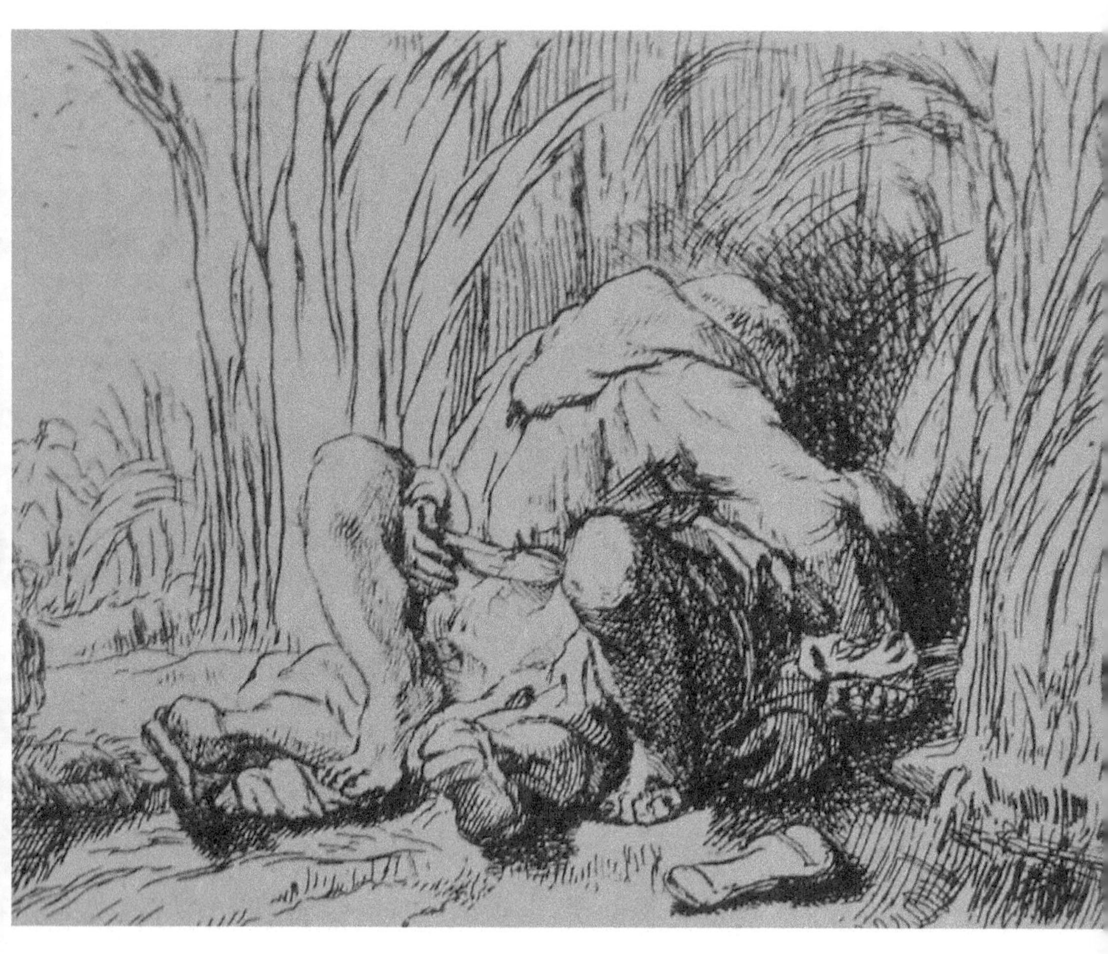

Rembrandt van Rijn, The Monk In the Cornfield

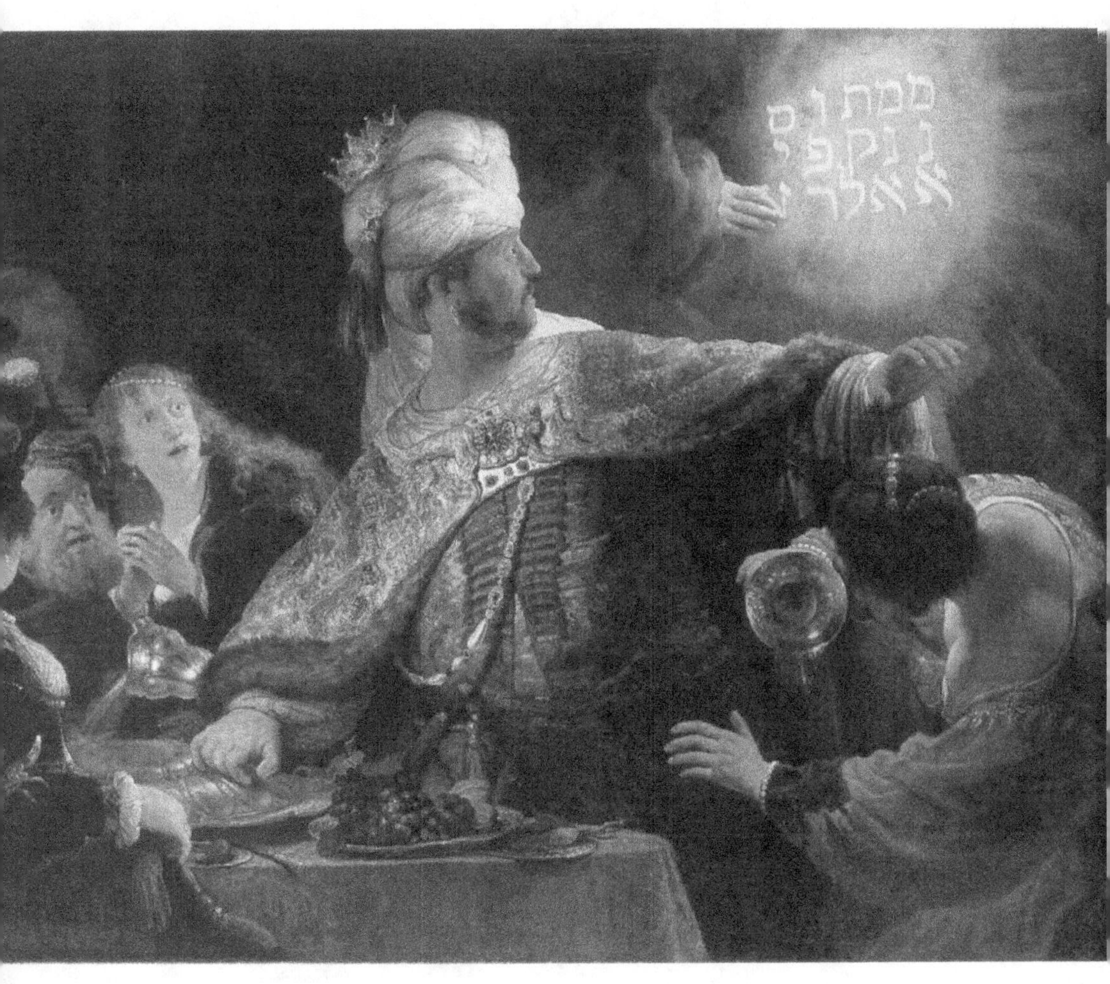

Rembrandt van Rijn, Belshazzar's Feast, 1635, National Gallery, London

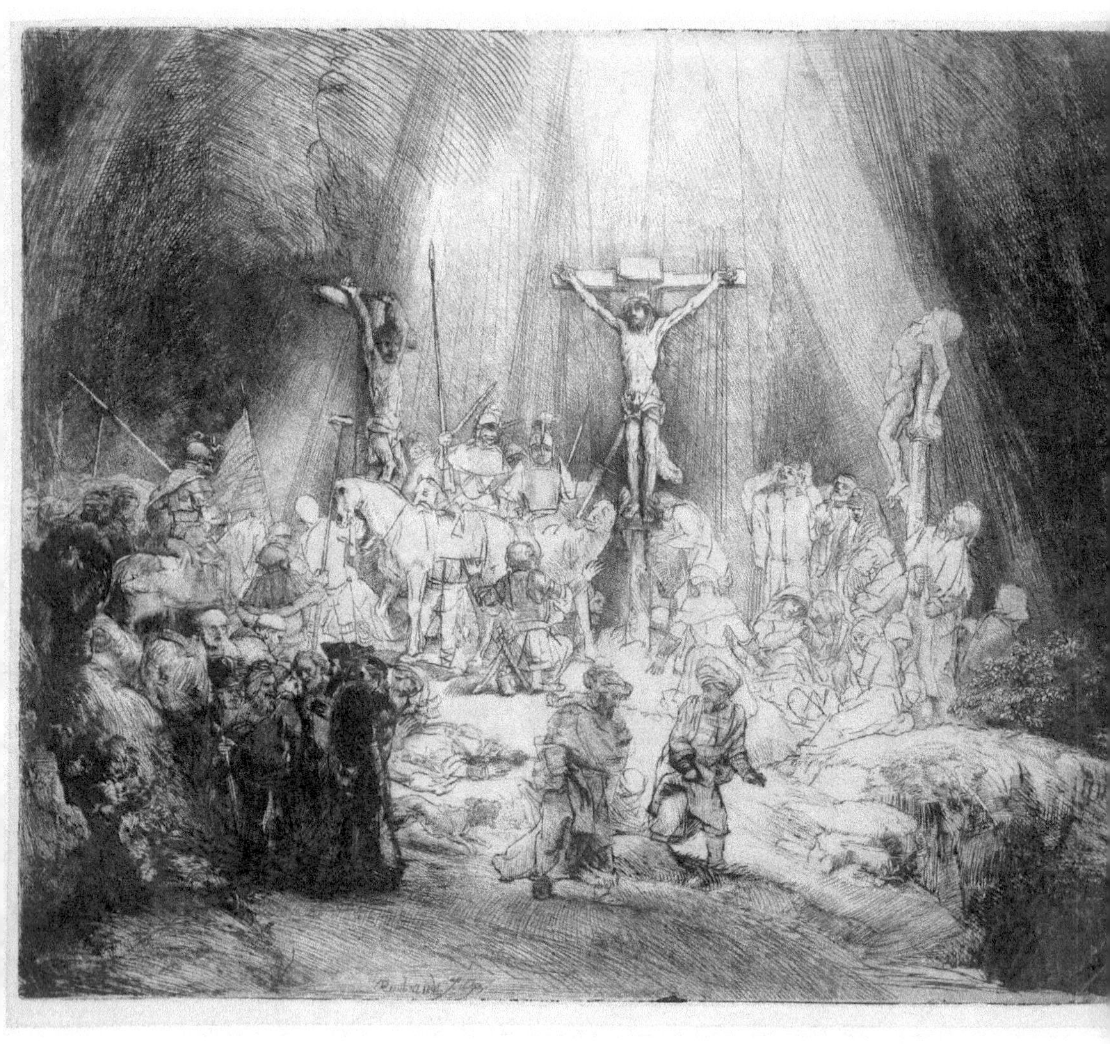

Rembrandt, The Three Crosses, 1653

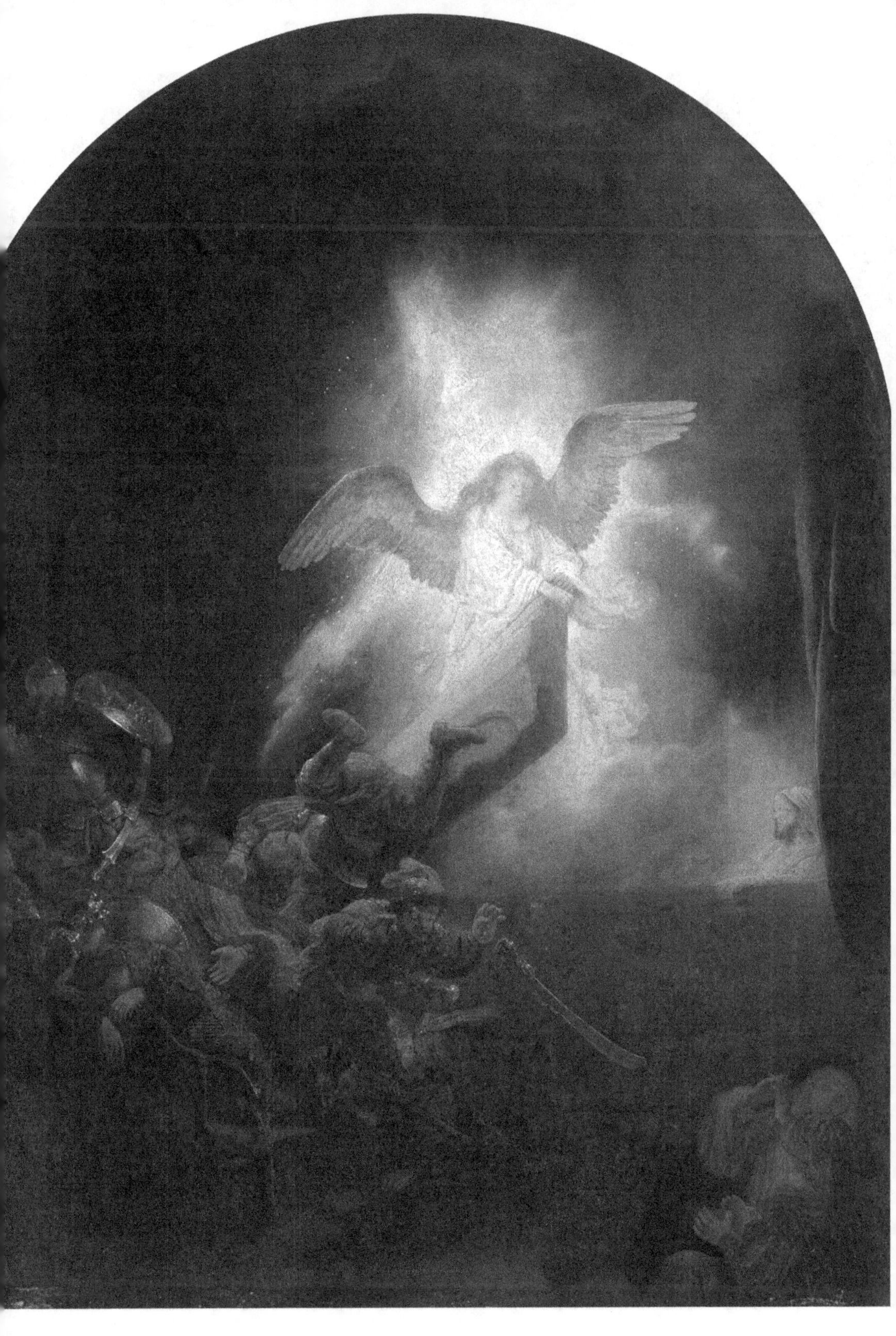

Rembrandt, The Resurrection

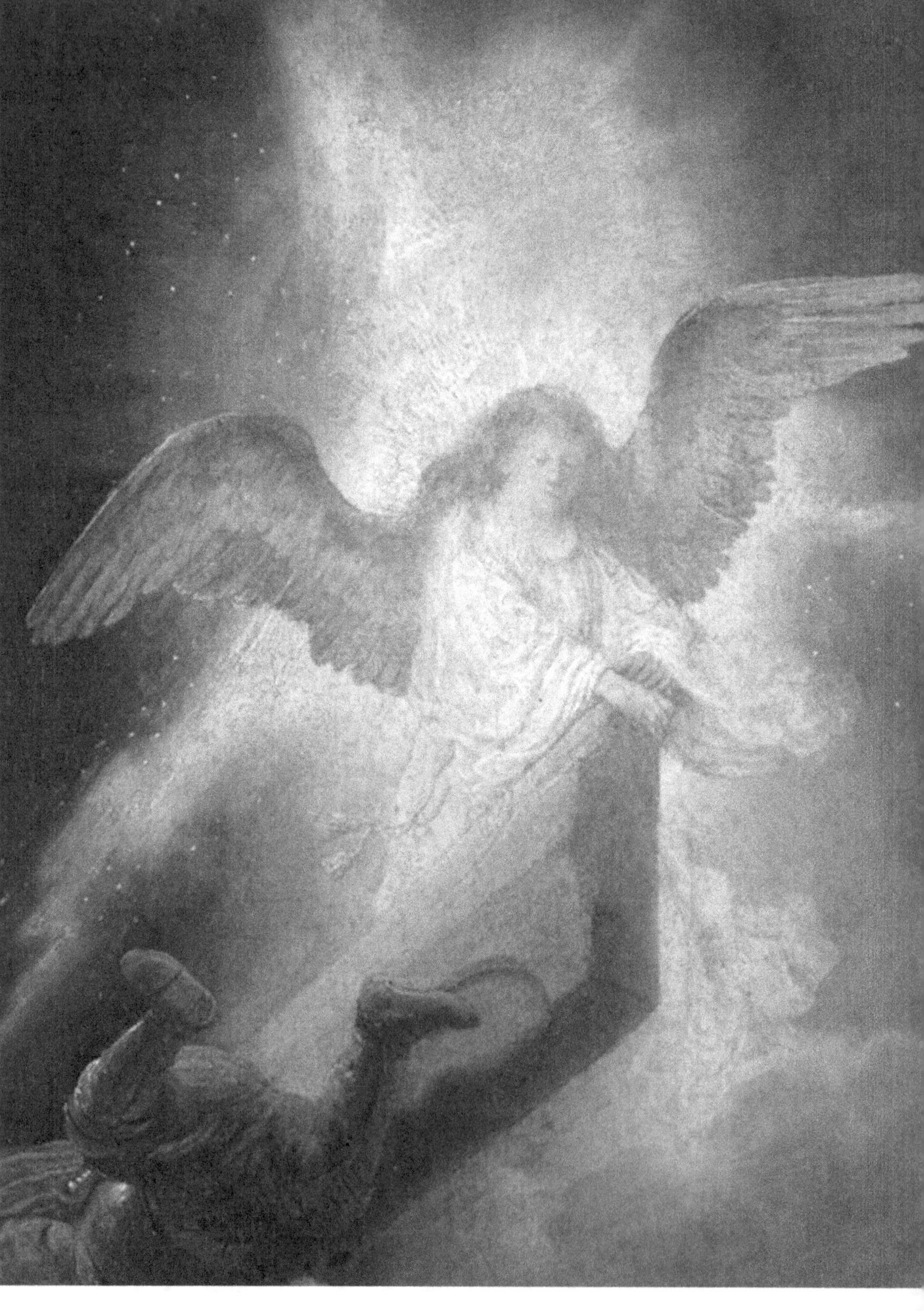

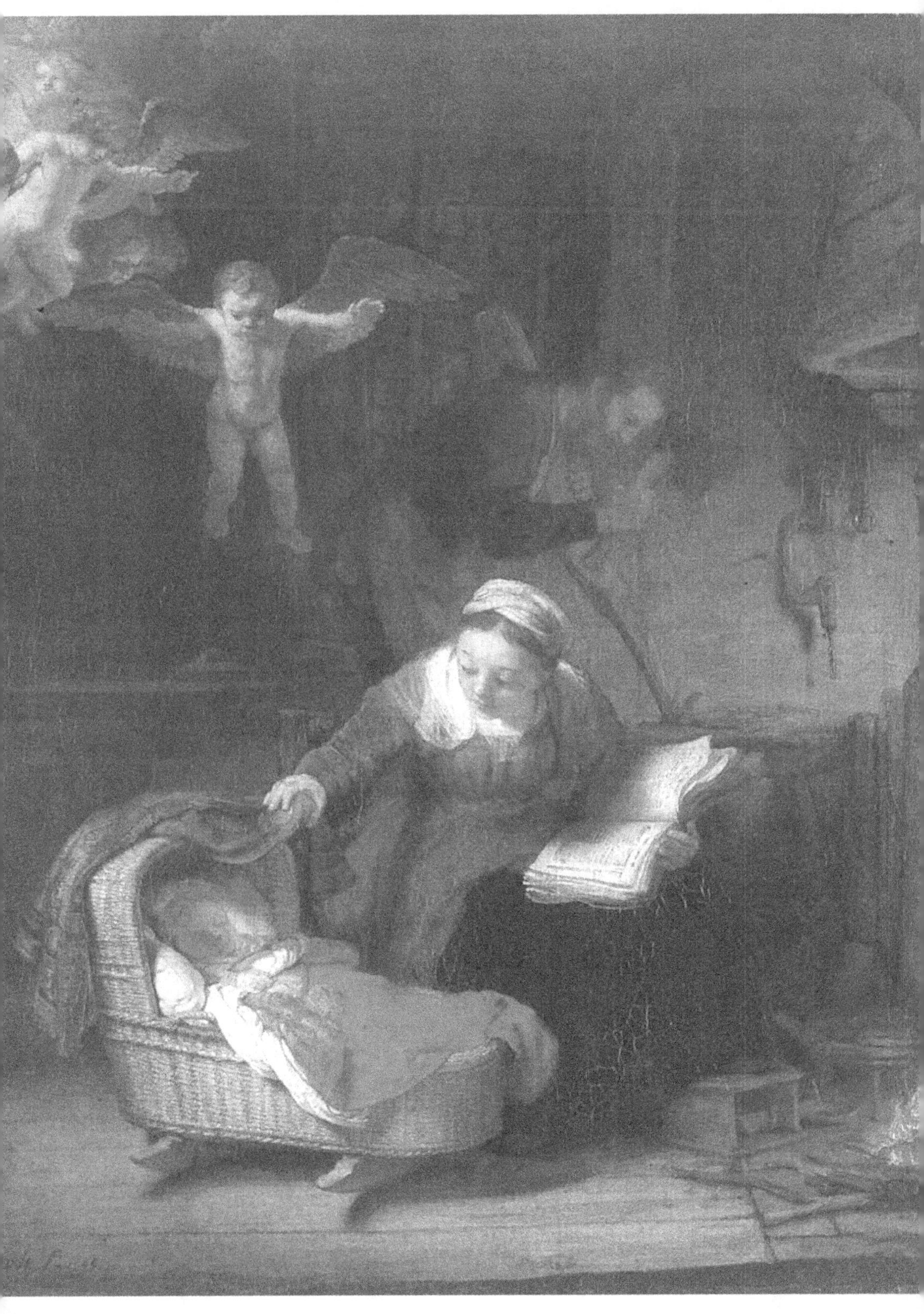

Rembrandt van Rijn, The Holy Family With Angels, 1645, Hermitage Museum

REMBRANDT AND HIS WORKS

The early pictures, in all ages, either merely indicate the character of bas-reliefs or single statues, – a cold continuity of outline, and an absence of foreshortening. The first move in advance, and that which constitutes their pictorial character, in contradistinction to sculpture, is an assemblage of figures, repeating the various forms contained in the principal ones, and thus rendering them less harsh by extension and doubling of the various shapes, as we often perceive in a first sketch of a work, where the eye of the spectator chooses, out of the multiplicity of outlines, those forms most agreeable to his taste. The next step to improvement, and giving the work a more natural appearance, is the influence of shadow, so as to make the outlines of the prominent more distinct, and those in the background less harsh and cutting, and consequently more retiring. The application of shadow, however, not only renders works of art more natural, by giving the appearance of advancing and retiring to objects represented upon a flat surface – thus keeping them in their several situations, according to the laws of aërial perspective – but enables the artist to draw attention to the principal points of the story, and likewise to preserve the whole in agreeable form, by losing and pronouncing individual parts. Coreggio was the first who carried out this principle to any great extent; but it was reserved for Rembrandt, by his boldness and genius, to put a limit to its further application. Breadth, the constituent character of this mode of treatment, cannot be extended; indeed, it is said that Rembrandt himself extended it too far; for, absorbing seven-eighths in obscurity and softness, though it renders the remaining portion more brilliant, yet costs too much. This principle, however, contains the greatest poetry of the art, in contradistinction to the severe outline and harsh colouring of the great historical style.

COMPOSITION

To arrive at a true knowledge of the inventions and compositions of Rembrandt, it is necessary, in the first instance, to examine those of Albert Durer, the Leonardo da Vinci of Germany. The inventions of this extraordinary man are replete with the finest feelings of art, notwithstanding the Gothic dryness and fantastic forms of his figures. The folds of his draperies are more like creased pieces of paper than cloth, and his representation of the naked is either bloated and coarse, or dry and meagre. His backgrounds have all the extravagant characteristics of a German romance, and are totally destitute of aërial perspective; yet, with the exception of the character of the people and scenery of Nuremburg, he is not more extravagant in his forms than the founder of the Florentine school, and had he been educated in Italy, he in all probability would have rivalled Raffaelle in the purity of his design. In his journal, which he kept when he travelled into the Netherlands, he mentions some prints he sent to Rome, in exchange for those he expected in return, and it is mentioned that Raffaelle admired his works highly. The multitude of his engravings, both on copper and wood, which were spread over Germany, influenced, in a great degree, the style of composition of those artists who came after him, and accordingly we see many points of coincidence in the compositions of Rembrandt. A century, however, had opened up a greater insight into the mysteries of painting than either Leonardo da Vinci or Albert Durer ever thought of; one alone, – viz. aërial perspective, seems to mark the line between the ancient and modern school; for though Durer invented several instruments for perfecting lineal perspective, his works exhibit no attempt at giving the indistinctness of distant objects. To Rubens, Germany and Holland were indebted for this essential part of the art, so necessary to a true representation of Nature. This great genius, in his contemplation of the works of Titian and others, both at Venice and in Madrid, soon emancipated the art of his country from the Gothic hardness of Lucas Cranach, Van Eyck, and Albert Durer; but notwithstanding his taste and knowledge of what constituted the higher qualities of the Italian school, the irregular combinations and multitudinous assemblage of figures found in the early German compositions remained with him to the last. His works are like a melodrama, filled with actors who have no settled action or expression allotted them, while in the works of Raffaelle, and other great composers, the persons introduced are limited to the smallest number necessary to explain the story. This condensing of the interest, if I may use the expression, was borrowed originally from the Greeks, of whose sculptures the Romans availed themselves to a great degree. On the other hand, this looseness of arrangement, and what may be termed ornamental, not only spread through Germany, but infected the schools of Venice; witness the works of Tintoretto and Paul Veronese, in which the expression of the countenance absolutely goes for nothing, and the whole arrangement is drawn out in a picturesque point of view, merely to amuse and gratify the eye of the spectator.

Now, with all these infectious examples before him, Rembrandt has done much to concentrate the action, and reduce the number drawn out on the canvas to the mere personages who figure in the history. Witness his "Salutation of the Virgin," in the Marquis of Westminster's collection, which is evidently . engendered from the idea contained in the design of Albert

Durer. His strict application to nature, while it enabled him to destroy the unmeaning combinations of his predecessors, led him into many errors, by the simple fact of drawing from the people in his presence. But are not others chargeable with some incongruities? Are the Madonnas of Murillo anything but a transcript of the women of Andalusia? The women of Venice figure in the historical compositions of Titian and Paul Veronese, and the Fornarina of Raffaelle is present in his most sacred subjects; those, therefore, who accuse Rembrandt of vulgarity of form, might with equal justice draw an invidious comparison between classic Italian and high Dutch. In many of his compositions he has embodied the highest feeling and sentiment, and in his study of natural simplicity approaches Raffaelle nearer than any of the Flemish or Dutch painters. Of course, as a colourist and master of light and shade, he is all powerful; but I allude, at present, to the mere conception and embodying of his subjects on this head.

Fuseli says, – "Rembrandt was, in my opinion, a genius of the first class in whatever relates not to form. In spite of the most portentous deformity, and without considering the spell of his *chiaro-scuro*, such were his powers of nature, such the grandeur, pathos, or simplicity of his composition, from the most elevated or extensive arrangement to the meanest and most homely, that the best cultivated eye, the purest sensibility, and the most refined taste, dwell on them equally enthralled. Shakspere alone excepted, no one combined with so much transcendent excellence so many, in all other men unpardonable, faults, – and reconciled us to them. He possessed the full empire of light and shade, and of all the tints that float between them; he tinged his pencil with equal success in the cool of dawn, in the noon-day ray, in the livid flash, in evanescent twilight, and rendered darkness visible. Though made to bend a steadfast eye on the bolder phenomena of nature, yet he knew how to follow her into her calmest abodes, gave interest to insipidity and baldness, and plucked a flower in every desert. None ever, like Rembrandt, knew how to improve

✳ 74

an accident into a beauty, or give importance to a trifle. If ever he had a master, he had no followers; Holland was not made to comprehend his power."

And in another lecture, speaking of the advantage of a low horizon, he says: – "What gives sublimity to Rembrandt's Ecce Homo more than this principle? a composition which, though complete, hides in its grandeur the limits of its scenery. Its form is a pyramid, whose top is lost in the sky, as its base in tumultuous murky waves. From the fluctuating crowds who inundate the base of the tribunal, we rise to Pilate, surrounded and perplexed by the varied ferocity of the sanguinary synod to whose remorseless gripe he surrenders his wand, and from him we ascend to the sublime resignation of innocence in Christ, and, regardless of the roar, securely repose on his countenance. Such is the grandeur of a conception, which in its blaze absorbs the abominable detail of materials too vulgar to be mentioned. Had the materials been equal to the conception and composition, the Ecce Homo of Rembrandt, even unsupported by the magic of its light and shade, or his spell of colours, would have been an assemblage of superhuman powers."

Reynolds, in his Eighth Discourse, speaking of the annoyance the mind feels at the display of too much variety and contrast, proceeds to say: – "To apply these general observations, which belong equally to all arts, to ours in particular. In a composition, where the objects are scattered and divided into many equal parts, the eye is perplexed and fatigued, from not knowing where to find the principal action, or which is the principal figure; for where all are making equal pretensions to notice, all are in equal danger of neglect. The expression which is used very often on these occasions is, the piece wants repose – a word which perfectly expresses a relief of the mind from that state of hurry and anxiety which it suffers when looking at a work of this character. On the other hand, absolute unity, that is, a large work consisting of one group or mass of light only, would be as defective as an heroic poem without episode, or any collateral incidents to recreate the mind with that variety which it requires. An instance occurs to me of two painters (Rembrandt and Poussin) of characters totally opposite to each other in every respect, but in nothing more than in their mode of composition and management of light and shadow. Rembrandt's manner is absolute unity; he often has but one group, and exhibits little more than one spot of light in the midst of a large quantity of shadow: if he has a second mass that second bears no proportion to the principal. Poussin, on the contrary, has scarcely any principle mass of light at all, and his figures are often too much dispersed, without sufficient attention to place them in groups. The conduct of these two painters is entirely the reverse of what might be expected from their general style and character, the works of Poussin being as much distinguished for simplicity as those of Rembrandt for combination. Even this conduct of Poussin might proceed from too great affection to simplicity of another kind, too great a desire to avoid the ostentation of art with regard to light and shadow, on which Rembrandt so much wished to draw the attention; however, each of them ran into contrary extremes, and it is difficult to determine which is the most reprehensible, both being equally distant from the demands of nature and the purposes of art."

This unity is observable in the composition of Rembrandt; even where a multiplicity of figures are employed, they are so grouped that the masses of light and shade are interrupted as little as possible; and it is only in his earlier works, such as those now in the Munich Gallery, where this isolated light is carried to extravagance. In many of his later pictures, we have not only subordinate groups, but a repetition of the principal lights; also a greater breadth of half-tint. "Composition," says Reynolds, "which is the principal part of the invention of a painter, is by far the greatest difficulty he has to encounter. Every man that can paint at all, can execute individual parts; but to keep these parts in due subordination as relative to a whole, requires a comprehensive view of the art, that more strongly implies genius

✳ 76

than perhaps any other quality whatever." Now Rembrandt possessed this power in an eminent degree. At the revival of painting in Italy, the compositions consisted entirely of subjects taken from Sacred Writ – subjects that imposed a purity of thought and a primitive simplicity upon the artists; these qualities were, however, in a great measure lost in passing through the Venetian and German schools, where either the love for pictorial effect or the introduction of catholic ceremonies took precedence of every other arrangement. The prolific genius of Rubens spread this infectious mode of treatment through Flanders and Holland, till at length, in the hands of the painters of smoking and drinking scenes, historical subjects, even of a sacred character, became quite ridiculous. Yet, with all these examples of bad and vulgar taste around him, we find many compositions of Rembrandt less degraded by mean representation than many of the best of the works of the Venetian and Flemish painters. Take, for example, his design of Christ and his Disciples at Emmaus, the principal figure in which is certainly more refined than the Christ either in the pictures of Titian or Rubens of the same subject; in fact, the idea of it is taken from the Last Supper, by Raffaelle, (the Mark Antonio print of which he must have had.) Raffaelle is indebted for the figure to Leonardo da Vinci; and if we were to trace back, I have no doubt we should find that the Milanese borrowed it from an earlier master; indeed, we perceive in the progress of painting much of the primitive simplicity and uniformity preserved in the best works of the Italian school. It was only when composition passed through the prolific minds of such artists as Paul Veronese, Tintoretto, and Rubens, that it was made subservient to the bustle, animation, and picturesque effect of their works. When we find, therefore, any remains revived in the pictures of Rembrandt, who was surrounded by compositions of a vulgar and low cast, we can only ascribe it to the taste and genius of this great painter. In the design just mentioned, the idea of the Disciples, as if struck with astonishment and awe at the bursting forth of the divinity of Christ, is admirably conceived. As the heads are taken from the people of his country, they of necessity partake of the character of the people. This cannot be justified, though it is excusable. Reynolds, on this head, speaking of the ennobling of the characters in an historical picture, says, "How much the great style exacts from its professors to conceive and represent their subjects in a poetical manner, not confined to mere matter of fact, may be seen in the Cartoons of Raffaelle. In all the pictures in which the painter has represented the apostles, he has drawn them with great nobleness; he has given them as much dignity as the human figure is capable of receiving. Yet we are expressly told in Scripture they had no such respectable appearance; and of St. Paul in particular we are told by himself that his *bodily* presence was *mean*. In conformity to custom, I call this part of the art History Painting: it ought to be called Poetical, as in reality it is." He further adds, "The painter has no other means of giving an idea of the mind but by that external appearance which grandeur of thought does generally, though not always, impress on the countenance, and by that correspondence of figure to sentiment and situation which all men wish, but cannot command." As I cannot defend the mean appearance of the disciples, neither shall I exculpate our great artist from blame in introducing a dog into so grand a subject; we can only excuse him on the plea of following the practice of his predecessors. Titian, in his celebrated picture, has not only introduced a dog, but a cat also, which is quarrelling with the former for a bone under the table. To this love for the introduction of animals into their compositions, for the sake of picturesque variety, many of the greatest painters must plead guilty; and though the incongruity has been pointed out over and over again by the writers on art, it is still clung to as means of contrast with the human figure. In one of the sketches by the late Sir D. Wilkie for his picture of "Finding the Body of Tippoo Saib," he had introduced two dogs, and only obliterated them when informed that dogs were considered unclean by the people of the east, and therefore it was an impossibility for them to be in the palace of Seringapatam. While

I am upon this subject, it may not be amiss to refer to one of the
authorities who censures this practice. Fresnoy says, in his poem
on the "Art of Painting,"

"Nec quod inane, nihil facit ad rem sive videtur
Improprium miniméque urgens potiora tenebit
Ornamenta operis."

"Nor paint conspicuous on the foremost plain,
Whate'er is false, impertinent, or vain."
Mason.

On this rule, Reynolds remarks – "This precept, so obvious to
common sense, appears superfluous till we recollect that some
of the greatest painters have been guilty of a breach of it; for –
not to mention Paul Veronese or Rubens, whose principles as
ornamental painters would allow great latitude in introducing
animals, or whatever they might think necessary to contrast
or make the composition more picturesque – we can no longer
wonder why the poet has thought it worth setting a guard
against this impropriety, when we find that such men as
Raffaelle and the Caracci, in their greatest and most serious
works, have introduced on the foreground mean and frivolous
circumstances. Such improprieties, to do justice to the more
modern painters, are seldom found in their works. The only
excuse that can be made for those great artists, is their living
in an age when it was the custom to mix the ludicrous with
the serious, and when poetry as well as painting gave in to
this fashion."

Many of the compositions of Rembrandt indicate not only a
refined taste, but the greatest sensibility and feeling. For
example, the small etchings of the "Burial of Christ," and the
"Return from Jerusalem;" these, from their slightness, may lay
me under the same category as the old Greek, who, having a
house to sell, carried in his pocket one of the bricks as a sample;
yet, being his own indications, I have given them. It is worth
while to compare the "Entombment" with the same subject by

✳ 79

Raffaelle, in the Crozat Collection. The whole arrangement is treated in the finest taste of the Italian school. The other design has been always a favourite with the admirers of Rembrandt. The feeling character of the youthful Saviour is admirably portrayed. Holding his mother's hand, he is cheering her on her tiring journey, looking in her face with an expression of affection and solace; while she is represented with downcast eyes, fatigued and "pondering in her mind" the import of the words he had addressed to her, "How is it that ye sought me? wist ye not that I must be about my Father's business?" And even here we can almost excuse the introduction of the little dog, who, running before the group, is looking back, giving a bark of joy at their having found the object of their solicitude. The background is conceived in the finest spirit of Titian.

These are the touches of nature that, like the expressions of our own immortal Shakspere, however slight, and though dressed in modern garb or familiar language, reach the innermost sensibilities of the human heart.

The character and costume of the people, as well as the scenery of those subjects taken from Holy Writ, have been a matter of investigation both by artists and writers upon art; for although the events related in the New Testament are not of so ancient a date as those of the heathen writers, yet the mind seems to require that the style should be neither classic nor too strictly local. Hence, though the costume represented in the Venetian pictures is no doubt nearer the truth than that made use of by Raffaelle and other Italians, it fails to carry us back to ancient and primitive simplicity. The early pictures delineating Christian subjects are modelled upon Greek forms and dresses, and having been made the foundation of those works afterwards produced by the great restorers of painting, have gained a hold upon our ideas, which, if not impossible, is yet difficult to throw off. As the late Sir David Wilkie travelled into the East with the express purpose of painting the subjects mentioned in Scripture in more strict accordance with the people and their habits, it may be of advantage to give the student his opinions. In his Journal, he says – "After seeing with great attention the city of Jerusalem and the district of Syria that extends from Jaffa to the river Jordan, I am satisfied it still presents a new field for the genius of Scripture painting to work upon. It is true the great Italian painters have created an art, the highest of its kind, peculiar to the subjects of sacred history; and in some of their examples, whether from facility of inquiry or from imagination, have come very near all the view of Syria could supply. The Venetians, (perhaps from their intercourse with Cyprus and the Levant,) Titian, Paul Veronese, and Sebastian del Piombo, have in their pictures given the nearest appearance to a Syrian people. Michelangelo, too, from his generalizing style, has brought some of his prophets and sybils to resemble the old Jews about the streets of the Holy City; but in general, though the aspect of Nature will sometimes recall the finest ideas of Leonardo da Vinci and Raffaelle, yet these masters still want much that could be supplied here, and have a great deal of matters quite contrary to what the country could furnish. These contrarieties, indeed, are so great, that in discussions with the learned here, I find a disposition to that kind of change that would soon set aside the whole system of Italian and European art; but as these changes go too much upon the supposition that the manners of Scripture are precisely represented by the present race in Syria, it is too sweeping to be borne out by what we actually know. At the same time, there are so many objects in this country so perfectly described, so incapable of change, and that give such an air of truth to the local allusions of Sacred Writ, that one can scarcely imagine that these, had they been known to the painters of Italy, would not have added to the impressive power of their works. Without trying to take from the grand impression produced by the reading of the Sacred Writings, it may be said that from its nature many things must be confined to narrative, to description, to precept – and these are no doubt so strong as to supply to a pious mind everything that can be desired; but if these are to be represented,

✳ 81

as certainly they have been, by those of an art who have not seen Syria, it is clear some other country, Italy, Spain, or Flanders, will be drawn upon to supply this, and the reader of Scripture and the admirer of art will be alike deluded by the representation of a strange country in the place of that so selected and so identified as the Land of Promise – so well known and so graphically described from the first to the last of the inspired writers."

These remarks are certainly applicable, but only in a degree. What is quoted from Reynolds, in a former part, shows that a licence is indispensable; and yet, without destroying the apparent truth of the subject, many things are now established that, without their being facts, have taken such hold of our ideas that they cannot with safety be departed from. I may instance the countenances of our Saviour and the Virgin, as given by Raffaelle and Coreggio – we recognise them as if they had been painted from the persons themselves; I may also add the heads of the Apostles. With regard to the scenery, many circumstances may certainly be taken advantage of, always guarding against a topographical appearance that, by its locality, may prevent the work leading the spectator back into distant periods of time. Before quitting this part of the subject, which refers to Rembrandt's powers of composition, I may notice one or two of his designs, which stamp him as a great genius in this department of the art – viz., his "Christ Healing the Sick," "Haman and Mordecai," the "Ecce Homo," "Christ Preaching," and the "Death of the Virgin."

CHIARO-SCURO

From the position we are now placed in, surrounded by the accumulated talent of many centuries, it is easy to take a retrospective view of the progress of art; and it is only by so doing that we can arrive at a just estimate of the great artists who advanced it beyond the age in which they lived, and this seems mainly to have been achieved by a close observance of nature. As in philosophy the genius of Bacon, by investigating the phenomena of visible objects, put to flight and dissipated the learned dogmas of the school of Aristotle, so in sculpture the purity and simplicity of the forms of Phidias established a line of demarcation between his own works and those of the formal, symmetrical, and dry sculpture of his predecessors. Sculpture, till then, lay fettered and bound up in the severity of Egyptian Hieroglyphics. Likewise we perceive the genius of Michelangelo and Raffaelle setting aside the stiffness and profile character existing in the works of Signorelli and Masaccio. In Venice, Titian emancipated the arts from the grasp of Giovanni Bellini. In Germany, Rubens must be considered the great translator of art out of a dead language into a living one, to use a metaphor, and into one that, like music, is universal. Previous to Rembrandt, the pupils of Rubens had thrown off every affinity not only to Gothic stiffness, but even to that degree of regularity of composition which all classes of historical subjects require. Independent of Rubens and his pupils, we find Rembrandt was aware of the great advances made in natural representations of objects by Adrian Brauwer, (several of whose works, by the catalogue given of his effects, were in his possession;) therefore, as far as transparency and richness, with a truthfulness of tint, are concerned, Brauwer had set an example. But in the works of Rembrandt we perceive a peculiarity entirely his own – that of enveloping parts in beautiful obscurity, and the light again emerging from the shadow, like the softness of moonlight partially seen through demi-transparent clouds, and leaving large masses of undefined objects in darkness. This principle he applied to compositions of even a complicated character, and their bustle and noise were swallowed up in the stillness of shadow. If breadth constitutes grandeur, Rembrandt's works are exemplifications of mysterious sublimity to the fullest extent. This "darkness visible," as Milton expresses it, belongs to the great founder of the school of Holland, and to him alone. Flinck, Dietricy, De Guelder, and others his pupils, give no idea of it; their works are warm, but they are without redeeming cool tints; they are yellow without pearly tones; and in place of leading the eye of the spectator into the depths of aërial perspective, the whole work appears on the surface of the panel. There are none of those shadows "hanging in mid air," which constitute so captivating a charm in the great magician of chiaro-scuro; not only are objects of solidity surrounded by softening obscurity, but the contiguous atmosphere gives indications of the influence of the light and shade. To these principles the art is indebted for breadth and fulness of effect, which constitute the distinct characteristics between the early state and its maturity – and to Rembrandt we owe the perfection of this fascinating quality.

We must, nevertheless, always look back with wonder at what was achieved by Coreggio. Even when painting flourished under the guidance of Leonardo da Vinci and Giorgione, Reynolds, speaking of this quality in contradistinction to that of relief, says, "This favourite quality of giving objects relief, and which De Piles and all the critics have considered as a requisite of the greatest importance, was not one of those objects which much engaged the attention of Titian. Painters of an inferior rank have far exceeded him in producing this effect. This was a great object of attention when art was in its infant state, as it is at present with the vulgar and ignorant, who feel the highest satisfaction in seeing a figure which, as they say, looks as if they could walk round it. But however low I might rate this pleasure of deception, I should not oppose it, did it not oppose itself to a quality of a much higher kind, by counteracting entirely that fulness of manner which is so difficult to express in words, but which is found in perfection in the best works of Coreggio, and, we may add, of Rembrandt. This effect is produced by melting and losing the shadows in a ground still darker than those shadows; whereas that relief is produced by opposing and separating the ground from the figure, either by light, or shadow, or colour. This conduct of inlaying, as it may be called, figures on their ground, in order to produce relief, was the practice of the old painters, such as Andrea Mantegna, Pietro Perugino, and Albert Durer, and to these we may add the first manner of Leonardo da Vinci, Giorgione, and even Coreggio; but these three were among the first who began to correct themselves in dryness of style, by no longer considering relief as a principal object. As those two qualities, relief and fulness of effect, can hardly exist together, it is not very difficult to determine to which we ought to give the preference. An artist is obliged for ever to hold a balance in his hand, by which he must determine the value of different qualities, that when some fault must be committed, he may choose the least. Those painters who have best understood the art of producing a good effect have adopted one principle that seems perfectly conformable to reason – that a part may be sacrificed for the good of the whole. Thus, whether the masses consist of light or shadow, it is necessary that they should be compact and of a pleasing shape; to this end, some parts may be made darker and some lighter, and reflections stronger than nature would warrant. Paul Veronese took great liberties of this kind. It is said, that being once asked why certain figures were painted in shade, as no cause was seen in the picture itself, he turned off the inquiry by answering, 'Una nuevola che passa,' – a cloud is passing, which has overshadowed them."

Before entering more minutely into an investigation of the principles of Rembrandt with regard to chiaro-scuro, I must again revert to those of Coreggio. Opie, speaking of the method of this great artist, says, "To describe his practice will be in a great degree to repeat my observations on chiaro-scuro in its enlarged sense. By classing his colours, and judiciously dividing them into few and large masses of bright and obscure, gently rounding off his light, and passing, by almost imperceptible degrees, through pellucid demi-tints and warm reflections into broad, deep, and transparent shade, he artfully connected the finest extremes of light and shadow, harmonized the most intense opposition of colours, and combined the greatest possible effect with the sweetest and softest repose imaginable." Further on, he remarks – "The turn of his thoughts, also, in regard to particular subjects, was often in the highest degree poetical and uncommon, of which it will be sufficient to give as an instance his celebrated *Notte*, or painting of the 'Nativity of Christ,' in which his making all the light of the picture emanate from the child, striking upwards on the beautiful face of the mother, and in all directions on the surrounding objects, may challenge comparison with any invention in the whole circle of art, both for the splendour and sweetness of effect, which nothing can exceed, and for its happy appropriation to the person of Him who was born to dispel the clouds of ignorance, and diffuse the light of truth over a darkened world!" Now, this work Rembrandt must have seen, or at least a copy from it, as his treatment of the same subject, in the National Gallery, indicates; but the poetry is lost, for it would be impossible to imitate it without a direct plagiarism. It may, however, have given a turn to his thoughts, in representing many of his subjects under the influence of night in place of day, such as his "Taking down from the Cross," by torch light; his

✳ 86

"Flight into Egypt," with the lantern; the "Burial of Christ," &c. While other men were painting daylight, he turned the day into night, which is one of the paths that sublimity travels through. The general idea most people have of Rembrandt is, that he is one of the dark masters: but his shadows are not black, they are filled with transparency. The backgrounds to his portraits are less dark than many of either Titian or Tintoretto. His landscapes are not black, they are the soft emanations of twilight; and when he leads you through the shadows of night, you see the path, even in the deepest obscurity. As colour forms a constituent part of chiaroscuro, I must, in this division, confine myself more particularly to black and white, both in giving examples from his etchings, and explaining the various changes he made upon them in order to heighten the effect. The etching I have here given is the "Nativity," in the darkest state; in the British Museum there are no less than seven varieties, and the first state is the lightest. But in order to render his mode of proceeding more intelligible, I shall explain the progress of his working. His first etchings are often bit in with the aquafortis, when the shadows have but few ways crossed with the etching point: these are often strongly bit in, that, when covered over with finer lines, the first may shine through, and give transparency. In the next process he seems to have taken off the etching ground, and laid over the plate a transparent ground, (that is to say, one not darkened by the smoke of a candle;) upon this he worked up his effect by a multiplicity of fresh lines, often altering his forms, and adding new objects, as the idea seemed to rise in his mind. After which, when the plate was again subjected to the operation of the acid, the etching ground was removed, and the whole worked up with the greatest delicacy and softness by means of the dry needle, to the scratches of which the aquafortis is never applied. This process it is that gives what is termed the *burr*, and renders the etchings of Rembrandt different from all others. Now this *burr* is produced, not by the ink going into the lines, but by the printer being obstructed in wiping it off by the raised edge which the dry point has forced up; for when these lines run through deep shadows, we often see that they print white, from the ink being wiped off the top of the ridge.

This is the foundation of what is called mezzotint engraving, which I shall notice in another place. By keeping these remarks in mind, we shall easily perceive how it is that so many variations occur in impressions from his plates, depending entirely on the direction in which the printer wiped off the ink – whether across the ridges, or in the same direction as the lines. Varieties have also arisen from these ridges wearing away by the friction of the hand; and as Rembrandt's copper plates, judging from those I have examined, were soft, they soon wore down. We also find this dark effect given in many of his varieties by merely leaving the surface partially wiped, and touching out the high lights with his finger, or a piece of leather. These impressions must have been taken by himself, or, at least, under his superintendence. Several of his plates are worked on with the graver, such as his "Taking down from the Cross;" but that evidently is by the hand of an engraver. We see the same in several of the etchings of Vandyke, but their value decreases as the finishing extends.

While we are upon the subject of his etchings, it will, perhaps, be of use to confine the conduct of his chiaro-scuro to his etchings alone, as his treatment is very different to what he adopted when he had colour to deal with; and in this respect he must have been influenced by the example of Rubens and Vandyke, proofs of all the engravings after whose pictures we perceive he had in his possession. In order that we may more clearly understand the reason of many of his etchings remaining unfinished in parts, while other portions are worked up with the greatest care, I shall give an extract from the Journal of Sir Joshua Reynolds, when in Flanders. In describing a picture in the Church of the Recollets, at Antwerp, he says: – "Over the altar of the choir is the famous 'Crucifixion of Christ between two Thieves,' by Rubens. To give animation to this subject, he has chosen the point of time when an executioner is piercing the side of Christ, whilst another, with a bar of iron, is breaking the limbs of one of the malefactors, who, in his convulsive agony, which his body admirably expresses, has torn one of his feet from the tree to which it was nailed. The expression in the action of this figure is wonderful. The attitude of the other is more composed, and he looks at the dying Christ with a countenance perfectly expressive of his penitence. This figure is likewise admirable. The Virgin, St. John, and Mary the wife of Cleophas, are standing by, with great expression of grief and resignation; whilst the Magdalen, who is at the feet of Christ, and may be supposed to have been kissing his feet, looks at the horseman with the spear with a countenance of great horror. As the expression carries with it no grimace or contortion of the features, the beauty is not destroyed. This is by far the most beautiful profile I ever saw of Rubens, or, I think, of any other painter. The excellence of its colouring is beyond expression. To say that she may be supposed to have been kissing Christ's feet, may be thought too refined a criticism; but Rubens certainly intended to convey that idea, as appears by the disposition of her hands, for they are stretched out towards the executioner, and one of them is before and one behind the cross, which gives an idea of their having been round it. And it must be remembered that she is generally represented as kissing the feet of Christ: it is her place and employment in those subjects. The good Centurion ought not to be forgotten – who is leaning forward, one hand on the other, resting on the mane of his horse, while he looks at Christ with great earnestness. The genius of Rubens nowhere appears to more advantage than here; it is the most carefully finished picture of all his works. The whole is conducted with the most consummate art. The composition is bold and uncommon, with circumstances which no other painter had ever before thought of – such as the breaking of the limbs, and the expression of the Magdalen; to which we may add the disposition of the three crosses, which are placed perspectively, in a very picturesque manner – the nearest bears the thief whose limbs they are breaking; the next the Christ, whose figure is straighter than ordinary, as a contrast to the others; and the furthermost the penitent thief. This produces a most interesting effect, but it is what few but such a daring genius as Rubens would have attempted. It is here, and in such compositions, that we properly see Rubens, and not in little pictures of Madonnas and Bambinos. It appears that Rubens made some changes in this picture after Bolswert had engraved it. The horseman who is in the act of piercing the side of Christ holds the spear, according to the print, in a very tame manner, with the back of the hand over the spear, grasping it with only three fingers, the forefinger lying straight over the spear; whereas, in the picture, the back of the hand comes *under* the spear, and he grasps it with his whole force. The other defect, which is remedied in the picture, is the action of the executioner who breaks the legs of the criminal: in the print, both of his hands are over the bar of iron, which makes a false action; in the picture, the whole disposition is altered to the natural manner in which every person holds a weapon which requires both hands – the right is placed over, and the left under it. This print was undoubtedly done under the inspection of Rubens himself. It may be worth observing, that the keeping of the masses of light in the print differs much from the picture; this change is not from inattention, but design; a different conduct is required in a composition with colours from what ought to be followed *when it is in black and white only.* We have here the authority of this great master of light and shadow, that a print requires more and larger masses of light than a picture. In this picture, the principal and the strongest light is the body of Christ, which is of a remarkably clear and bright colour. This is strongly opposed by the very brown complexion of the thieves, (perhaps the opposition here is too violent,) who make no great effect as to light; the Virgin's outer drapery is dark blue, and the inner a dark purple, and St. John is in dark strong red. No part of these two figures is light in the picture but the head and hands of the Virgin, but in the print, they make the principal mass of light of the whole composition. The engraver has certainly produced a fine effect, and I suspect it is as certain that if this change had not been made, it would have appeared a black and heavy print. When Rubens thought it necessary, in the print, to make a mass of light of the drapery of the Virgin and St. John, it was likewise necessary that it should be of a beautiful shape, and be kept compact; it therefore became necessary to darken the whole figure of the Magdalen, which in the picture is at least as light as the body of Christ; her head, linen, arms, hair, and the feet of Christ, make a mass as light as the body of Christ. It appears, therefore, that some parts are to be darkened, as well as other parts made lighter. This, consequently, is a science which an engraver ought well to understand before he can presume to venture on any alteration from the picture he means to represent. The same thing may be remarked in many other prints by those engravers who were employed by Rubens and Vandyke; they always gave more light than they were warranted by the picture – a circumstance which may merit the attention of engravers."

As most of these engravings were made from studies in black and white, perhaps reduced from the picture by the engraver, but certainly touched on afterwards by the painters themselves, they form a school for the study of light and shade when deprived of colour. In the etchings of Rembrandt, therefore, we ought to bear in mind that splendour of effect was what he aimed at, and the means adopted by Rubens and Vandyke were carried still further by the fearless master of chiaro-scuro. Now that the eye has been accustomed to engravings where the local colour is rendered, when we look over a folio of the works of Bolswert, Soutman, Pontius, and others of the Flemish engravers, they appear, notwithstanding their overpowering depth and brilliancy, unfinished, from the lights of the several coloured draperies and the flesh tones being left white. They also occasionally look spotty in effect, from the extreme strength of the shadows and black draperies. In Rembrandt's works these defects are avoided, by finishing his darks with the greatest care and softness, while the figures in the light masses are often left in mere outline: the lights are also reduced in size as they enter the shade; while the darks in the light portions of his prints are circumscribed to a mere point, for the purpose of giving a balance and solidity. The shadows of the several objects likewise assume a greater delicacy as they enter into the masses of light. In these respects, the Hundred Guilder print is a striking example.

As we are now considering light and shade when unaccompanied by colour, I may notice that those portions where the dark and light masses come in contact are the places where both the rounding of the objects by making out the forms, and also the patching down the half-tint with visible lines, may be followed out with the greatest success, as it prevents the work being heavy in effect, and also assists the passage of the light into the shadow. The quality of the lights and darks is flatness. The Flemish engravers seem to have been very particular in the method of producing their shadow, both with regard to the direction of the lines, and also their repetition; their object seems to have been intenseness of dark with transparency of execution. In a conversation with Sir Thomas Lawrence upon the subject of shadows, his ideas were that they ought to be as still as possible, and that all the little sparkling produced by the crossing of the lines ought to be extinguished, or softened down. In painting, his notions were that they ought to be kept cool. Without presuming to differ with so excellent an artist, it is but proper to mention that all the best engravers, from the time of Bolswert to our own, are of a contrary opinion; and our best colourists, from Coreggio to Rembrandt, and from Rembrandt to Wilkie, were diametrically opposite in their practice. As far as engraving is concerned, it is but fair to notice that Lawrence had Rembrandt on his side, of whose works he was a great admirer.

I may appear to have dwelt too long upon this subject of engraving, but as the etchings of Rembrandt form so large a portion of his popularity, we cannot enter too minutely into the various sources of their excellence. I shall now proceed to describe the etching of "Doctor Faustus," a copy of which I have given.

Some think that it represents Fust, the partner of Guttenburg, who, by his publication of Bibles in Paris, was looked upon by the people as a dealer in the black art. The papers hung up by the side of the window look like the sheets of his letter-press, and the diagram that attracts his attention, and rouses him from his desk, indicates by words and symbols a connexion with Holy Writ. But the general opinion is, that it is Dr. John Faustus, a German physician, in his study. This Dr. Faustus was supposed to have dealings with familiar spirits, one of which has raised this cabalistic vision, that enters the window with overwhelming splendour, like the bursting of a shell, communicating its radiance to the head and breast of the figure, and, descending by his variegated garment, is extended in a spread of light over the whole lower part of the composition. The light of the window being surrounded by a mass of dark, receives intense importance, and is carried as far as the art can go. It is also, I may observe, rendered less harsh and cutting by its shining through the papers at the side, and by the interruption of the rays of the diagram. The light passing behind the figure, and partially thrown upon a skull, gives an awe-striking appearance to the whole; while the flat breadth of light below is left intentionally with the objects in mere outline. This etching seems never to have been touched on from the first impressions to the last – the first state is dark with excess of burr; the last is merely the burr worn off.

Before quitting this subject, I wish to make a few remarks. It has been said by some of Rembrandt's biographers, that he made alterations in his prints for the sake of enhancing their value; but we know by experience that every alteration he made, however it might be for the better, struck off a certain portion of its money value. I believe his desire to better the effect was the only incitement. Many were improved by his working upon them after the first proofs, and many were deteriorated in effect; but every additional line at the least struck off a guilder. I have mentioned that in this etching the brilliancy of the light in the window is enhanced by its being surrounded by a mass of dark; but the same advantage would have accrued from its extension by a mass of half light, as it would then have had a greater breadth of soft light. This subject was a great favourite with the late Sir David Wilkie, and he introduced this window in his picture of "The School;" but this being a light composition, he treated it in the way I have mentioned above. It was a common practice with Wilkie to adopt some part of a celebrated work as a point to work from, and carry out his design upon this suggestion. The spectator, by this means, was drawn into a predisposition of its excellence, without knowing whence it had arisen. Thus, in his "John Knox Preaching," there are many points of similarity with the "St. Paul Preaching," by Raffaelle. I may also mention here what we often perceive in the works of Rembrandt – in place of having the light hemmed in by a dark boundary, it is spread out into a mass of half-light; and the same treatment is adopted with regard to his extreme darks, they communicate their properties to the surrounding ground. These qualities are the foundation of breadth and softness of effect.

These observations may appear iterations of what has been mentioned before – but truths get strengthened by being placed in new positions. In dividing a work of this kind into portions, it is difficult to give a preference to any department, especially with such an artist as Rembrandt, who was equally celebrated in all – and I have only given a priority to historical subjects as they hold a higher rank than portraiture. But his portraits are those productions of his pencil which are most peculiar to himself.

PORTRAIT OF THE BURGOMASTER SIX

This is the most finished and perfect of all the etchings of Rembrandt; and as it was done expressly for his friend and patron, we can easily imagine that the painter exerted himself to the utmost, so as to render it worthy of the subject. I have been at some trouble to get an account of the family of Jan Six, but have gleaned little from those books connected with the history of Holland. During the war with England, in the reign of Charles the Second, he was Secretary of State to the City of Amsterdam, and his family was afterwards connected with some of their most celebrated men. But what has rendered his name more famous than intermarrying with the families of Van Tromp or De Ruyter, is his patronage of Rembrandt – in the same way that Lord Southampton's name is ennobled by his patronage of Shakspere. We know he was devoted to literature as well as the fine arts, having left a tragedy on the story of Medea, a copy of which is mentioned in the catalogue of Rembrandt's effects, and an etching by the artist was prefixed to the work – viz., the "Marriage of Jason and Creusa;" the rare states of this print are before the quotation of the Dutch verses underneath – also the statue of Juno is without the diadem, which was afterwards added. I have mentioned that this portrait was a private plate; in fact, the copper is still in the possession of the family. In a sale which took place in

1734, for a division of the property among the various branches, fourteen impressions were sold, but brought comparatively small prices, from the number to be contended for. Two proofs, however, on India paper are still in the portfolio of his descendants, which in five years will, it is said, be brought to the hammer, as by that time the parties will be of age. These proofs will in all probability realize two hundred guineas each. The ease and natural attitude of the figure in this work are admirable: the intensity of the light, with the delicacy and truth of the reflected lights, are rendered with the strong stamp of genius; the diffusion of the light also, by means of the papers on the chair, and the few sparkling touches in the shadow, completely take this etching out of the catalogue of common portraiture. The only work I can at present think of that can be brought into competition with it, is the full-length portrait of Charles the First, by Vandyke, in the Queen's Collection, and which is rendered so familiar by Strange's admirable engraving.

In entering into an examination of the execution of this print, it is evident the whole effect is produced by means of the dry point, which must have been a work of great labour. The best impressions are on India paper; and I perceive, by referring to Gersaint's catalogue, that at the sale of the Burgomaster's property, they only brought about eighteen florins. The next portrait amongst his etchings that at all approaches to the Burgomaster, is that of "Old Haring," which has always struck me as one of the foundations for the style of Sir Joshua Reynolds in portraiture. A fine impression of this work, on India paper, is more like Sir Joshua than many prints after his own pictures; and with all the high veneration I have for Reynolds, I cannot omit noticing how very ambiguously he frequently speaks of this great genius. We know his master, Hudson, had an excellent collection of Rembrandt's works, and therefore he must have been early imbued with their merits and peculiarities. This, however, we shall have a better opportunity of noticing when we come to the treatment of colour. The next etching in excellence I should mention is the "Portrait of John Lutma, the Goldsmith," with the light background; this was afterwards softened down by the introduction of a window. And here I must observe, that though he often had light backgrounds to his prints, yet in his finished pictures they were generally the reverse. The etching of "Ephraim Bonus, the Jewish Physician," is also one of his most effective works; the introduction of the balustrade, on which he leans descending the staircase, removes it from the ordinary level of mere portraiture. On the hand that rests upon the balustrade, is a ring, which in the very rare impressions, from its being done with the dry point, prints dark from the burr. These are invaluable, as in that state the whole work has the fulness and richness of a picture. A very large sum was given for the impression of the print in this state – now in the British Museum – in fact, one hundred and sixty pounds; though at the Verstolke sale, where this print was purchased, the commission given amounted to two hundred and fifty pounds: but when we consider that the collection in the British Museum is now the finest in existence, no extra price should be spared to complete the collection, especially as these works are foundations for the sure improvement of the fine arts in the country. The crown jewels are exhibited as a necessary appendage to the rank of the nation – but there the value stops; now the works of art in this country are not only valuable, but intrinsically beneficial. We know that Charles the Second pawned the crown pearls to the Dutch for a few thousands; but our collection of Rembrandts would realize in Holland at least ten thousand pounds. This, of course, is a digression, and is merely mentioned here to show how absurd the hue and cry is, that the country is wasting money in purchasing a few specimens of fine art. The "Portrait of Utenbogardus" is also excellent; and I may here notice the large book, which Rembrandt was so fond of introducing, as a means of a breadth of light and employment for his portraits. Now, to these circumstances we are indebted for some of the finest works of both Reynolds and Lawrence: amongst many, I might mention the large ledger in

Lawrence's "Portraits of the Baring Family," and Sir Joshua's picture of the "Dilettante Society," and others. No doubt we find these means of making up a picture both in Raffaelle and Titian; but it is rendered more applicable to our own purposes when it is brought nearer to our own times, especially when translated by so great a genius as Rembrandt. The next fine work amongst his etchings is the "Portrait of Cornelius Silvius," the head of which, being delicately finished with the dry needle, is seldom seen very fine. This also has a book, and the hand extended beyond the frame of the oval opening, upon which it casts its shadow. This practice of representing objects nearer the eye than the frame is certainly to be observed in some of the prints after Rubens and others, and has descended to several common prints in our own time, but ought not to be adopted, as bordering too much upon that art which may be designated as a sort of *ad captandum vulgus* display. As we shall speak more particularly of Rembrandt's portraits when colour is investigated, these works are merely mentioned as excellent specimens of composition and chiaro-scuro. I must not omit, however, to notice here the great Coppenol, the writing-master to the city of Amsterdam: he holds a pen and a sheet of paper in his hand, and is looking at the spectator with a look of intelligent observation. The head and figure of this work were perfected, in the first instance, before the background was put in, and in this state is exceedingly rare – the one in the British Museum is valued at five hundred guineas, and was left, amongst other rare works in his collection, by the Rev. Mr. Cracherode, to the public. And here we ought to bear in mind, when individuals contribute so largely by their bequests to the country, it is our bounden duty to carry out their views by perfecting the various collections as opportunities offer in the course of time, which to them was impossible. In one of the impressions in the Museum, in a finished state, is written, in a large ornamental hand, a commendation by Coppenol himself, wherein he says he does so to unite his name with that of the great artist, Rembrandt Van Ryn, as by that means he knows he shall secure immortality to himself. The portrait, however, that is the most powerful, as well as the most rare, is Van Tolling the Advocate. The effect, both from the reflected light on the face, and the fearless masses of burr, is more like a picture than a print, and renders every other etching comparatively tame. From the chemical bottles at the side, and from the character of the gown in which he is dressed, I am of opinion that he was a physician. The excellence of this work, added to its rarity, has at all times produced large prices. There are two states of this print – the first with an irregular beard, the second with the beard cut square, also some additional work on the drapery, &c.; but, what is worthy of remark is, in both states it is exceedingly scarce; in fact, there are but seven impressions known – viz., two in the British Museum, one in Mr. Holford's collection, one in Mr. Hawkins', in Amsterdam one, in Paris one, and one in the collection of Mr. Rudge. I ought here to notice that the Van Tolling is one of the prints bequeathed to the nation by the Rev. Mr. Cracherode, and that at the sale of the Hon. Pole Carew's prints, in 1835, this valuable etching was purchased for the late Baron Verstolke, for two hundred and twenty pounds.

I shall now enter upon an investigation of the Landscapes of Rembrandt, which, equally with his portraits, are quite peculiar to himself, but differing from all others not from any eccentricity of manner, but from their giving the real essence and character of the scene, when denuded of any trifling and extraneous matters. Whatever Rembrandt touched was impressed with the peculiar characteristics of his genius; hence it is that the smallest stroke in his etchings is pregnant with truth. Though painting belongs exclusively to no country, but represents the natural appearance of each, still it is reserved for genius alone to be able to perceive and place on canvas the essence, as it were, or great leading features of the subject. I am now more particularly speaking of landscape scenery. In all countries and climates there are peculiarities of effect, which, however interesting to the traveller, or a source of investigation to the philosopher or man of science, yet are necessarily excluded from the recording pencil of the artist; his appeal is to mankind at large, not to the isolated few who observe but one side of the subject. The true artist looks upon nature as the chameleon, capable of giving out any variety, and yet all equally true; hence it is that the skies, for example, of Claude, Salvator Rosa, and Gaspar Poussin are universally subordinate to the general effect of the picture. These men, living in Italy, were quite aware of the various prismatic effects observable in sunset, but were also convinced of the necessity of making the sky subservient, at least conducive to, the breadth and harmony of the picture. It may be said that Titian and Tintoretto embodied the deep and intense blues of the Venetian atmosphere, but we may remark that their skies are always held in check by the deep reds and browns of the draperies of their figures. Let us now, however, turn our remarks more immediately to Rembrandt, and the scenery and effects observable in Holland. Any one conversant with the pictures of the Dutch school must have observed peculiar features in the skies of Backhuysen, Cuyp, and Rembrandt, arising entirely from the localities of the scenes of their several pictures. My young friend, E. W. Cooke, long a resident in Holland, and a keen and observing artist, remarked that the skies in the pictures of Backhuysen, though dark and inky, were precisely what we see now – the deep Zuyder Sea swallowing up any refraction of light which would otherwise have illuminated the clouds; while the skies of Cuyp, receiving the coruscations arising from the meeting of the two rivers, the Meuse and the Waal, the scenes of most of his pictures, exhibit that luminous reflection and unsteady appearance peculiar to his works. I mention these matters, not to prove that these great observers of nature followed implicitly what was presented to their observation, but to show that when even copying the peculiar character of natural phenomena, it was done with a strict reference to the harmony of their works, and made subservient to one great broad principle. In a flat country like Holland, especially where a low horizontal line is chosen, we perceive a peculiar feature takes precedence of everything else –

that is, the quick diminution of those lines which run to the point of sight, whilst the lines running parallel with the base line of the picture retain their length in a greater degree; hence the accumulation of these lines, such as the division of fields, &c., gradually shade down the distant parts of the landscape, while the foreshortened lines assume the appearance of so many spots, or dark touches. In Rembrandt we perceive this character faithfully rendered, and also, assisted by his judicious management, the lines, such as the banks of canals or roads, as they reach the foreground, are strongly pronounced, by either bringing them in contact with strong light, or giving them breadth and force by enriching them with broken ground, reeds, or dark herbage. The objects that stand up, such as trees, &c., are enlarged and darkened as they approach the eye; thus not only enabling them to keep their situation, but also to assist the perspective effect in the highest degree. His small landscape etchings illustrate these remarks, and are full of the touches of truth and nature; and where objects are wanting to give variety and interest, he introduces masses of shadow, or dark clumps of trees, leaving other parts in mere outline. The love of his art caused him to be always provided with the materials for drawing and etching, so that we have these transcripts of nature fresh from the fountain head. We know this from an anecdote mentioned by Daulby. In describing the etching of "Six's Bridge," in his catalogue, he says, "This plate was produced by an incident which deserves to be related. Rembrandt lived in great intimacy with the Burgomaster Six, and was frequently at his country seat. One day, when they were there together, the servant came to acquaint them that dinner was ready, but as they were sitting down to table, they perceived that mustard was wanting. The Burgomaster immediately ordered his servant to go into the village to buy some. Rembrandt, who knew the sluggishness of the Dutch servants, and when they answer *austons* (a-coming) they are half an hour before they appear, offered the Burgomaster a wager that he would etch a plate before his man returned with the mustard. Six accepted the wager, and Rembrandt, who had always plates at hand ready varnished, immediately took one up, and etched upon it the landscape which appeared from the window of the parlour in which they were sitting. The plate was finished before the servant returned, and Rembrandt won his wager. The etching is slight, but it is a wonderful performance, considering the circumstance that produced it." It is not wonderful on account of the rapidity with which it was done, but the genius and science that pervade every touch, not only in the general arrangement, but in the judicious management of the smallest darks; they are all in the most effective situations. When the plate was bit in, the name was left out; it was afterwards added with the dry point; also a little shading was given to the hat of one of the figures on the bridge, which in the rare state is white. I may notice here that it was also Rembrandt's practice to sketch with the dry point alone, as several of his landscapes show; this has a very rich and full effect. His most finished and striking landscape is perhaps the etching of the "Three Trees." What I have said respecting his giving force to those parts nearest the eye, may be seen in the strong dark under the platform of the mill – which etching I have given, as it has always been considered the mill in which he was born; but I believe it is merely a mill of a picturesque character, which he consequently etched. In the rare impressions, the sky is much stained on the plate towards the house and mill, and I believe intentionally so, as it enables the subject to melt more softly into the background, by the outline being less harsh; at least, I found in my copy, when the person employed to clean the margin of the plate cleaned the stains in the sky also, that I had to restore them. As it will be necessary to go over the ground again with regard to Rembrandt's landscapes, when we enter upon an investigation of his principles of colour, I shall now commence upon that department, fully conscious how high he stands as an artist in that difficult branch of the art, at the same time aware how feeble words must be to express adequately the deep-toned richness of Rembrandt's colouring.

✳ 102

COLOUR

Perhaps, if we can comprehend a species of coloured chiaro-scuro, or the addition of colour to the broad and soft principles of light and shade, we shall be able to form a clear perception of the effects of Rembrandt's colouring. Indistinctness of tint, such as colours assume under the influence of twilight, is a strong characteristic of his manner – the shadows never so dark that a black or blue cannot tell firmly in the midst of them; with the total absence of all harshness, from the outlines of objects melting into their adjacent grounds, or assuming an importance after emerging from a mass of indefinite corresponding hues. As he has a mass of shadow with a mass of light, so he has an accumulation of warm colours in opposition to a congregation of cold – every combination introduced conducing to the great principles of breadth. When such is the plan upon which a work is laid down, we can easily perceive how powerfully the smallest touch of positive colour will tell – as in the midst of stillness a pin falling to the ground will be heard. Cuyp has this quality in a high degree, only on another scale – a uniformity of unbroken tone, and in masses of half-tint only, like a few sparkles of light touches, dealt out with the most parsimonious pencil, producing a glitter like so many diamonds. This it is that prevents a work from being heavy, for by their fewness they require not the aid of black grounds to give them consequence, and by their being touched upon colours of the same quality, they avoid the appearance of harshness; in fact, the principles of these two great artists were the same; only from the general tone of Cuyp's pictures being light, his strong darks tell with great power, and Rembrandt's half tints being of a low tone, his high lights become more forcible. I may here mention not only the breadth of Rembrandt's shadows, but their peculiar transparency and clearness, loose in the handling, and filled with air and space, whereas his lights are solid and firm – possessing not only the characteristics of nature in distinctiveness, but also in variety; and though we see always, on a general principle, light upon light and dark on a dark ground, yet we perceive inroads made upon each by their several antagonists; hot and cold colours darting into each other's provinces. This practice is also conducive to breadth, for tints of different hues may be interspersed both in the darks and lights, provided they are of equal strength with those adjoining them. We may observe in Rembrandt – that those colours introduced into the shadows are more under the influence of indistinctness, while those in the light are brighter; this is quite a deviation from the Roman school, where the colours are pronounced so harshly as to set the influence of chiaro-scuro at defiance.

Barry, in his sixth lecture, speaking of colours, says – "The happy effects of those sure and infallible principles of light and colour which Rubens had so successfully disseminated in the Netherlands, were soon found in every department of art. Landscapes, portraits, drolls, and even the dullest and most uninteresting objects of still life, possess irresistible charms and fascination from the magic of those principles. Rembrandt, who, it is said, was never at Venice, might, notwithstanding, have seen, without going out of his country, many pictures of the Venetian school. Besides, he was about thirty years younger than Rubens, whose works were a general object of study when Rembrandt was forming himself. But, however it be, there is no doubt, for the colouring and chiaro-scuro, Rembrandt is one of the most able artists that ever lived. Nothing can exceed the beauty, freshness, and vigour of his tints. They have the same truth, high relish, and sapidity as those of Titian. Indeed, they have the closest resemblance to the hues of Titian when he had Giorgione most in view. There is identically the same attention to the relievo and force obtained by his strong shadows and low deep tones; and his chiaro-scuro, though sometimes too artificial, is yet often (particularly in contrasted subjects) productive of the most fascinating effects. In the tones of Rembrandt, though we recognise the same richness and depth as in Giorgione and Titian, yet there is a suppleness and lifelike character in his flesh unlike either, both from his manner of handling, and also his hot and cold tints being less blended."

The late Sir David Wilkie, in one of his letters, speaking of the death of Sir Thomas Lawrence, says – "I do not wonder at the impression made among you in Rome by the death of Sir Thomas Lawrence; here, it engrossed for a time every other pursuit. One of the last remarks he made to me indicated his extreme admiration of Sir Joshua Reynolds, who, he thought, had, with Rembrandt, carried the imitation of nature, in regard to colours, further than any of the old masters." In many of the higher qualities of colour and chiaro-scuro, Reynolds comes nearer to Rembrandt than any other artist who has succeeded him.

Reynolds, in his lectures, speaking of Gainsborough, observes – "We must not forget, whilst we are on this subject, to make some remarks on his custom of painting by night, which confirms what I have already mentioned – his great affection to his art, since he could not amuse himself in the evening by any other means so agreeable to himself. I am, indeed, much inclined to believe that it is a practice very advantageous and improving to an artist, for by this means he will acquire a new and higher perception of what is great and beautiful in nature. By candlelight, not only objects appear more beautiful, but from their being in a greater breadth of light and shadow, as well as having a greater breadth and uniformity of colour, nature appears in a higher style, and even the flesh seems to take a higher and richer tone of colour. Judgment is to direct us in the use to be made of this method of study; but the method itself is, I am very sure, advantageous. I have often imagined that the two great colourists, Titian and Coreggio, though I do not know that they painted by night, formed their high ideas of colouring from the effects of objects by this artificial light. But I am more assured that whoever attentively studies the first and best manner of Guercino will be convinced that he either painted by this light, or formed his manner on this conception."

How far Coreggio may have formed his principles upon the effects of lamplight it is impossible to decide, seeing that, though his shadows have great breadth, yet his lights have more of a phosphorescent character, tinged, as it were, with the coolness of moonlight; but Titian has all the glow of this property, or, as Reynolds remarks, "as if he painted with the sun shining into the room." The Italian pictures of Vandyke have much of this phosphorescent character – whereas many of those he painted in England have more of a daylight appearance. With regard to Rembrandt, he seems to have regulated the entire scheme both of his chiaro-scuro and colour, on this foundation: his many paintings, drawings, and etchings of candlelight subjects, show how much his taste led to this class of art; and his daylight pictures, from the warmth of colour and breadth of shadow, proclaim the source from which he derived the cause of their brilliancy and force. From the light being tinged with yellow, the half-tone partakes of the same warmth, which gives a greenish tint even to his grey tones. This conduct conveys an emanation of the principal light passing over the more delicate shadows. In his daylight subjects it is not so; the light being often comparatively cool, is allowed to extend its influence to the secondary lights, and then, as it subsides into the shadow, is led in by the dark being lighted up by touches of red and brown; thus the light touches in the dark are warm, though the high light and secondary are cool. In Coreggio we often find the shadows more hot than even in Rembrandt, from his principal light and secondary being more cool. Rembrandt never allows his lights, even though comparatively cool, to pass into the shadow without a few touches of warm colour; this was the practice of Rubens, to enrich, as it were, "the debateable land." When this principle of painting candlelight subjects fell into the hands of his pupils, the harmony and colouring of the whole were lost or changed. For example, Hoogstraten, his pupil, instructed Schalcken, as did also Gerard Dow; but the candlelight pieces of Schalcken are hot and foxy, without any redeeming grey tones. When he painted by candlelight, he placed his sitter in a dark room, with a light, while he painted in another apartment, having a hole cut through the door to communicate with his sitter; the consequence was, the effect gave exactly what we see in such cases – a red, dull treatment of colour. We know these facts by an anecdote told of William the Third. When Schalcken was over in England, the King wished to sit to him for his portrait, and hearing of his celebrity in candlelight pieces, wished it painted under that effect. The painter placed a light in his Majesty's hand, and retired into the outer room; the candle guttering, kept dropping on the King's hand, but being unwilling to disturb the artist, the King held on, while the painter, intent on his work, proceeded without noticing it. Many of our English artists paint by gaslight; but the tones of the flesh are not benefited, gas shedding a white cool light compared with lamplight.

The practice of painting by candlelight originated neither with Rembrandt nor Gainsborough; in fact, we find that all academies, from the time of Bacio Bandinelli to our own, were always opened at night, both for the purposes of drawing and painting. But these effects generally remain where they originated, and are seldom taken advantage of without the walls, the figure alone being considered, without reference to the background. Tintoretto was one of the first to apply the principles to his practice. Fuseli, speaking of chiaro-scuro, says – "The nocturnal studies of Tintoretto, from models and artificial groups, have been celebrated; those prepared in wax or clay he arranged, raised, suspended, to produce masses, foreshortening, and effect.

It was thence he acquired that decision of chiaro-scuro, unknown to more expanded daylight, by which he divided his bodies, and those wings of obscurity and light by which he separated the groups of his composition; though the mellowness of his eye nearly always instructed him to connect the two extremes by something that partook of both, as the extremes themselves by the reflexes with the background or the scenery. The general rapidity of his process, by which he baffled his competitors, and often overwhelmed himself, did not, indeed, always permit him to attend deliberately to this principle, and often hurried him into an abuse of practice which in the lights turned breadth into mannered or insipid flatness; and in the shadows into a total extinction of parts. Of all this he has in the schools of San Rollo and Marco given the most unquestionable instances – 'The Resurrection of Christ,' and 'The Massacre of the Innocents,' comprehend every charm by which chiaro-scuro fascinates its votaries. In the vision, dewy dawn melts into deep but pellucid shade, itself sent or reflected by celestial splendour and angelic hues; whilst in the infant massacre of Bethlehem, alternate sheets of stormy light and agitated gloom dash horror on the astonished eye."

Rembrandt, like Tintoretto, never destroyed the effective character of his chiaro-scuro by the addition of his colour, but made it a main contributor to the general character of the subject; hence that undisturbed and engulphing breadth which pervades his works. Fuseli, in the same lecture, defends the Venetian school from being considered as the "ornamental school." After selecting several of the pictures of Titian, as proofs of his grand and solemn specimens of colour, he thus proceeds – "But perhaps it is not to Titian, but to Tintoretto and Paul Cagliari, that the debaucheries of colour, and blind submission to fascinating tints, the rage of scattering flowers to no purpose, are ascribed. Let us select from Tintoretto's most extensive work in the Scuola of San Rocco, the most extensive composition, and his acknowledged masterpiece – 'The Crucifixion,' and compare its tone with that of Rubens and

Rembrandt of the same subject. What impression feels he who for the first time casts a glance over the immense scenery of that work? a whole whose numberless parts are connected by a lowering, mournful, minacious tone. A general fearful silence hushes all around the central figure of the Saviour suspended on the cross, his fainting mother, and a group of male and female mourners at its foot – a group of colours that less imitate than rival nature, and tinged by grief itself; a scale of tones for which even Titian offers me no parallel – yet all equally overcast by the lurid tone that stains the whole, and like a meteor hangs in the sickly air. Whatever inequality or dereliction of feeling, whatever improprieties of commonplace, of local and antique costume, the master's rapidity admitted to fill his space, and they are great, all vanish in the power which compresses them into a single point, and we do not detect them till we recover from our terror."

The picture of Rubens which we oppose to Tintoretto was painted for the Church of St. Walburgha, at Antwerp, after his return from Italy, and has been minutely described and as exquisitely criticised by Reynolds: "Christ," he says, "is nailed to the cross, with a number of figures exerting themselves to raise it. The invention of throwing the cross obliquely from one corner of the picture to the other, is finely conceived, something in the manner of Tintoretto." So far Reynolds. "In Tintoretto," says Fuseli, "it is the cross of one of the criminals they attempt to raise, who casts his eye on Christ, already raised. The body of Christ is the grandest, in my opinion, that Rubens ever painted; it seems to be imitated from the Torso of Apollonius, and that of the Laocoon. How far it be characteristic of Christ, or correspondent with the situation, I shall not here inquire; my object is the ruling tone of the whole – and of this the criticism quoted says not a word, though much of local colour, and grey and ochry balance. Would so great a master of tone as Reynolds have forgot this master-key if he had found it in the picture? The fact is, the picture has no other than the painter's usual tone. Rubens came to his work with gay, technic exultation, and by the magic of his pencil changed the horrors of Golgotha to an enchanted garden and clusters of flowers. Rembrandt, though on a smaller scale of size and composition, concentrated the tremendous moment in one flash of pallid light. It breaks on the body of Christ, shivers down his limbs, and vanishes on the armour of a crucifix – the rest is gloom."

This is given with all the eloquence Fuseli was so well able to utter; but it displays, also, a severe castigation on those who would class Tintoretto and Paul Veronese in the catalogue of ornamental painters. The observations which seem to have kindled his wrath are to be found in Sir Joshua's fourth lecture, in which he says – "Tintoretto, Paul Veronese, and others of the Venetian school, seem to have painted with no other purpose than to be admired for their skill and experience in the mechanism of painting, and to make a parade of that art which, as I before observed, the higher style requires its followers to conceal." But, to understand the matter, the whole lecture must be read. With regard to the two pictures Fuseli brings into comparison with the Venetian, both are described in Reynolds' Tour to Flanders and Holland. Sir Joshua certainly criticizes the Rubens correctly with regard to colouring; but sentiment it has none. The Rembrandt is now in the Munich Gallery, and though one of his early pictures, it is very grand and striking. Of it Reynolds remarks – "There are likewise in this room eight Rembrandts, the chief merit of which consists in his peculiarity of manner – of admitting but little light, and giving to that little a wonderful brilliancy. The colouring of Christ in the elevation of the cross cannot be exceeded – it is exactly the tint of Vandyke's 'Susanna,' in the other room; but whether the ground of this picture has been repainted, or the white horse, which was certainly intended to make the mass of light broader, has lost its brightness, at present the Christ makes a disagreeable mass of light."

In bringing the opinions of these two great artists in contact, the truth is elicited, that the tone of colour has much to do in conveying the sentiment and pathos of the picture, and

Rembrandt possessed this quality in a very high degree. In the infancy of the arts, when practised by rude nations, we find harsh and bright colours predominate in a very strong scale – in fact, the brighter the more effective on the uneducated eye; and it is only when the arts advance towards perfection that a subdued tone of colour is demanded as most compatible with refinement. Colour, both as an imitative quality, and also as an adjunct towards assisting the character of his subject, seems always to have been uppermost in Rembrandt's mind. His drawing, it is true, is open to censure, but his colour will stand the most searching investigation, and will always appear more transcendent the more it is examined. Reynolds, in his Journey through Holland, mentions a picture by Rembrandt, in the collection of the Prince of Orange – "a study of a Susanna, for the picture by Rembrandt which is in my possession: it is nearly the same action, except that she is here sitting. This is the third study I have seen for this figure – I have one myself, and the third was in the possession of the late Mr. Blackwood. In the drawing which he made for this picture, which I have, she is likewise sitting; in the picture, she is on her legs, but leaning forward. It appears extraordinary that Rembrandt should have taken so much pains, and have made at last so very ugly and ill-favoured a figure; but his attention was principally directed to the colouring and effect, in which it must be acknowledged he has attained the highest degree of excellence." The small picture in the National Gallery is a study of the same figure. Colour was the ruling principle with Rembrandt, the Alpha and Omega, in the same way that Richard Wilson designated the three qualifications for landscape painting, as contained in one – viz., *breadth*. The tones of colour with which Rembrandt clothed his subjects are always in the highest degree appropriate and conducive to the sentiment, whether within the "solemn temples," or the personification of some great supernatural event. As most of his historical subjects are from Sacred Writ, he never loses sight of those qualities which take them out of the page of every-day occurrences. I shall mention two, though one is sufficient for a master-key to them all. In the picture of "The Adoration of the Magi and Kings," in the Queen's Collection, the solemnity is carried to the utmost extent, like the mysterious leaf of a sybil's book; the only light shed over the scene seems to descend from the lurid rays of the star that stood over the place of the nativity, and guided them to the spot. To acquire the greatest breadth, he has placed the Virgin and child in the corner of the picture, and low down at the base, with the same feeling that impelled Shakspere, in his Constance, to utter, "Here is my throne, bid kings come bow to it." The presentation of incense and precious perfumes, of diadems and jewels, by crowned heads and venerable magi, not only removes the attendants to the background, but even Joseph is represented as wrapt in thought, and viewing from the shade the solemnity of the scene. The whole colouring of this work is in accordance with this feeling – subdued, except in the smallest portions of each hue, and these shine out like sparkling of jewels in a dark recess.

The other work I would particularize is, "The Salutation of the Virgin," in the collection of the Marquis of Westminster. This picture, though of small dimensions, yet exemplifies the peculiarity of Rembrandt's mode of treatment. Being less decided in the chiaro-scuro and tone of colour than the Wise Men's Offering, it is more difficult to describe; this also arises from the exquisite weaving in of the hot and cold colours. Having had it under my eye for a couple of months, I can easily recall it on the least effort of the memory; but to bring it before the spectator who has not seen it, and by no other art than the medium of words, is as difficult as it would be to bring an harmonious arrangement of music by a different means – one must be seen and the other heard to render an explanation evident, which even then can only be understood by connoisseurs in painting and music. I must therefore avail myself of technicalities, which may seem out of place, where we are investigating the general hue of the picture. It is divided into hot and cold colours, which are brought in contact in the centre – Elizabeth being clothed in red and yellow, the Virgin in blue, white, and cool grey. The hot colour is carried across by the red sleeve of Elizabeth, and part of her yellow shawl, and descends to the petticoat of a Negress who is removing the grey mantle from the Virgin, and is further extended by a few warm-coloured stones and touches in the pavement. The cool colour is carried past the warm tone of Zacharias and the porch above him by means of a grey green pillar, a peacock, and a few touches of cool colour on a bush at one corner of the warm side of the picture. The general tone of the work is of a low, deep hue, so that even the cool tints are not cold or raw, but a deep-toned brightness pervades the whole. Through the dark grey sky, that seems to descend to overshadow the group, a gleam of light darts upon the scene, as a connecting link between heaven and earth, and giving force and truth to the expression of Elizabeth, when she pronounces the words, "Blessed art thou among women, and blessed is the fruit of thy womb." The light that shoots through the gloom has roused a pea-hen and chicks, who shake off their sleep as if it was the dawn of day.

This is a very imperfect description, but will, nevertheless, serve to show the fine feeling and deep intent of the genius of Rembrandt. To extend this investigation further would be perhaps superfluous, did we not know that, even in our own time, doubts are entertained of the proper introduction of pictorial arrangements of chiaro-scuro and colour; but the grand style, like all other modes of portraying a work, must be made subservient to affecting the feelings of the spectator. I shall only bring two pictures in contrast to elucidate this principle still further – "The Burning of the Books at Ephesus," by Sebastian Bourdon; and "The Martyrdom of St. Lawrence," by Titian. As Bourdon has been considered the French Raffaelle, it is but fair that he should be taken as a follower of that school, devoted to composition and correct drawing, to the absence of all inferior qualities; the consequence is, he has represented the scene in mid-day, where the flames are red without extending their influence to surrounding objects; consequently, they are not luminous, nor conveying the idea of destruction. Titian, on the contrary, has chosen the darkness of night to represent the horrors of the martyrdom – the red burning light of the living coal conveys a tenfold force to the torments of the saint, and the very reality of the colour gives a corresponding truth to the scene, which takes it completely out of the regions of apocrypha, and stamps it with the character of Holy Writ. The descent of the cool light from heaven upon the scorching body of St. Lawrence is like a rush of water to counteract his sufferings, and give him a confidence in his future reward, which the spectator fully enters into. These are the triumphs that appropriate chiaro-scuro and colour achieve for their introduction into historical works.

That we may more clearly perceive the rank which Rembrandt holds as a colourist, I shall endeavour to investigate the peculiar qualities that characterise the several manners of Titian, Rembrandt, and Reynolds – the one living before, the other after our artist, and of course confining the investigation to portraiture alone. I have selected Titian in preference to Vandyke, not that I consider him, in this branch, superior; on the contrary, I agree with Sir Joshua, in mentioning Vandyke as the greatest portrait painter that ever existed, all things considered – but I wish to confine myself exclusively to colour, and in this branch it is evident that these three great artists are more similar in their works than any other painters; but Titian, by the concurrent testimony of his contemporaries and all succeeding judges upon the subject, is the highest authority on the great leading principles of colour. Besides, his works are in many instances uninjured by the rough usage of uneducated men. With regard to the works of Rembrandt, which are in comparison as of yesterday, many of them remain in the same frames and on the same walls on which they were first hung. The works of Reynolds, though of a more recent date, have suffered more, not from the ruthless hand of the picture-cleaner, but from his making use of more perishable materials. Still, from the variety of his vehicles, changed from an anxiety to get a nearer approach to the look and appearance of nature, many of his pictures are sufficiently perfect to build an investigation upon. Previous to the appearance of Giorgione and Titian, this branch of the art differed but little from the treatment the several heads received in historical pictures generally; only with this exception, that when introduced as the component parts of a work where a story had to be told, they were imbued with action and expression; but when treated as simple portraiture, the higher qualities were left out, and a quiet map of the face, to use a familiar expression, was all that was desired to be transferred to the canvas. Neither did the head receive that superiority over every other subordinate part of the work which science and a long line of celebrated examples seem now so imperatively to demand.

In drawing a comparison between the three great portrait painters, it is necessary, in the first instance, to refer to the several characters of their models, or sitters. The nobility of Venice were, at the time of Titian, men of long descent, dignified, and holding high rank in a city at that time the emporium of the merchandize of the East, and distributors of rich manufactures to the whole of civilized Europe; hence that "senatorial dignity" which characterises his works, and the style and richness of costume so necessary to grandeur, and the historical air in his portraits. His sitters also possessed countenance and figure well calculated to engender and support the noblest character of painting. The sitters of Reynolds, notwithstanding the pomatumed pyramids of the female hair, or the stiff, formal curls of the male, which set every attempt to beautify the features at defiance, either by extension of the forms or harmonizing the several parts of the countenance, (serious obstacles to pictorial beauty,) were still in possession of that bland and fascinating look which distinguishes people of high breeding. In contrast with these we have to array the models of Rembrandt's painting-room – fat burgomasters, florid in complexion and common in feature; Jews and attornies; shipbuilders, and hard harsh-featured master mechanics. Independent of the models themselves, there is a congenial feeling created in the artist who associates with and has to represent them; we imperceptibly imbibe the manners of those we are in contact with, either advantageously or injuriously. From these few remarks we may perceive that the dignified attitude, the broad general tone of the countenance, though deep, yet rendered bright and luminous by the jetty blackness of the hair and beard, were all conducive to the creation of the style of Titian – a style that swallows up the varieties of minute tints in a general breadth. So in Reynolds, the absence of everything strong in expression or harsh in colour gave a refinement to the heads of his men, and a beauty to the faces of his females; and to this treatment all his sitters were subjected – so that even those heads, however deficient in the originals, came off his easel ladies and gentlemen. A subdued delicacy of expression and colour removes them from the common look of familiar life. Now, on the contrary, the very character and colour of Rembrandt's heads are pronounced with the strong stamp of flesh and blood – an exact representation of nature in an unsophisticated state. His handling, his manner of leaving the various tints, and the marking of minute parts, all conspire to give his works that appearance of truth unfettered with the attempt to elevate the general character at the expense of individuality.

The peculiarity of Titian's portraits, independent of the high character and simple and dignified attitude of the figure, is a careful and distinct modelling of the features, with the half-shadows, though not dark, yet never slurred over – which in other hands would produce heaviness; but Titian counteracts this by the intense darkness of his dresses and backgrounds, so that the features, often modelled with the firmness of sculpture, are rendered comparatively gentle by the treatment of the other parts of the picture. The portraits of Sir Joshua have this peculiarity, that however loaded and enriched in every part of the work, the head is kept smooth, and often thinly painted. The whole-length of "The Marquis of Granby," and "The Portrait of Mrs. Siddons," two of his finest pictures, are examples of this mode of treating the head. This has given rise to an anecdote, that Mrs. Siddons, looking at the picture when unfinished, begged Sir Joshua not to touch the head any more – and having promised her, he refrained, notwithstanding the richness and depth of the fearless glazings would seem to demand a corresponding force in the head. The truth is, that Reynolds seems always to have depended upon the small dark shadows to give solidity to his heads, without clogging them with colour or dark half-tints. The importance of thus refining upon the head may be perceived in the portrait of himself, painted *con amore*, and presented to the Dilettante Society, of which he was a member. The features, and, indeed, the whole head, depend upon the extreme darks; the judicious arrangement of these shadows not only gives a pictorial dignity to the work, from the stamp of science, but also, where the features in nature are either blunt or mean in themselves, draws off the attention of the spectator to higher qualities. Shadows are never mean, but are the stamps of truth rendered beautiful by taste and feeling. Independent of the advantage of dark touches giving delicacy to the features that produce them, there is a motion and life given by the vivacity and freedom of the handling, which cannot with safety be taken with the features themselves. This quality seems very early to have been Sir Joshua's greatest anxiety to acquire. In a remark respecting the pictures of a rival, John Stephen Liotard, whose only merit was a strong likeness, with great neatness of finish, Reynolds says – "The high-finished manner of painting would be chosen if it were possible with it to have that spirit and expression which infallibly fly off when the artist labours; but there are transient beauties which last less than a moment, and must be painted in as little time; besides, in poring long the imagination is fatigued, and loses its vigour. You will find nature in the first manner – but it will be nature stupid, and without action. The portraits of Holbein are of this high-finished manner; and for colouring and similitude what was ever beyond them? But then you see fixed countenances, and all the features seem to remain immoveable."

Northcote observes, "Of mere likeness in portraiture Reynolds thought very little, and used to say that he could instruct any boy that chance might throw in his way to paint a likeness in a portrait in half a year's time; but to give an impressive and a just expression and character to a picture, or paint it like Velasquez, was another thing. What we are all," he said, "attempting to do with great labour, he does at once."

Barry, speaking of Reynolds as a portrait painter, mentions the wretched state the art was in before his time, and how elevated it became from the manner Sir Joshua treated it. In continuation, he says – "In many of Titian's portraits the head and hands are mere staring, lightish spots, unconnected with either the drapery or background, which are sometimes too dark, and mere obscure nothings; and in Lely, and even in Vandyke, we sometimes meet with the other extreme of too little solidity, too much flickering and washiness. Sir Joshua's object appears to have been to obtain the vigour and solidity of the one, with the bustle and spirit of the other, without the excess of either; and in by far the greatest number of his portraits he has admirably succeeded. His portrait of Mrs. Siddons is, both for the ideal and the executive, the finest portrait of the kind perhaps in the world; indeed, it is something more than a portrait, and may serve to give an excellent idea of what an enthusiastic mind is apt to conceive of those pictures of confined history for which Apelles was so celebrated by the ancient writers. But this picture of 'Mrs. Siddons, or the Tragic Muse,' was painted not long since, when much of his attention had been turned to history; and it is highly probable that the picture of Lord Heathfield, the glorious defender of Gibraltar, would have been of equal importance, had it been a whole length; but even as it is – only a bust – there is great animation and spirit, happily adapted to the indications of the tremendous scene around him; and to the admirable circumstance of the key of the fortress, firmly grasped in his hand, than which imagination cannot conceive anything more ingenious and heroically characteristic. It is, perhaps, owing to the Academy, and to his situation in it, to the discourses which he biennially made to the pupils upon the great principles of historical art, and the generous ardour of his own mind to realize what he advised, that we are indebted for a few expansive efforts of colouring and chiaro-scuro which would do honour to the first names in the records of art." And speaking of the large historical work he painted for the Empress of Russia, he adds – "Nothing can exceed the brilliancy of light – the force and vigorous effect of his picture of 'The Infant Hercules strangling the Serpent;' it possesses all that we look for and are accustomed to admire in the works of Rembrandt, united to beautiful forms and an elevation of mind to which Rembrandt had no pretensions. The prophetical agitation of Tiresias and Juno, enveloped in clouds, hanging over the scene like a black pestilence, can never be too much admired, and are, indeed, truly sublime."

After such commendations, and from so high an authority, we might feel a diffidence in bringing forward the great founder of the Dutch school in competition with such artists as Titian and Reynolds, did we not know that the qualities of the chiaro-scuro and colour of Reynolds are founded on the deep tones of Rembrandt, who, as a colourist, takes his proper place between the two heads of the Venetian and English schools. How far Rembrandt was indebted for his principles of colour to the works of Titian, it is impossible to say; but many of his pictures bear a greater affinity to the last style of this great colourist than to any other painter. We perceive by the catalogue of his effects, that folios containing drawings by Titian, also prints after him, were in his possession. The luminous, rich tones of his flesh are more like Titian than Rubens or Vandyke, whose works he must have been familiar with; and while his backgrounds are less black and inky than those in the portraits of Titian and Tintoretto, they are also more broken, both in colour and execution, which prevents heaviness. His handling – which conveys from its dexterity and touch so lifelike an appearance – is not unlike that of Frank Hals, of whom Reynolds speaks so highly: – "In the works of Frank Hals, the portrait painter may observe the composition of a face,

✻ 119

the features well put together, as the painters express it, from whence proceeds that strong, marked character of individual nature, which is so remarkable in his portraits, and is not found in an equal degree in any other painter. If he had joined to this most difficult part of the art a patience in finishing what he so correctly planned, he might justly have claimed the place which Vandyke, all things considered, so justly holds, as the first of portrait painters." There is, however, this difference in their works – independent of the flesh of Rembrandt's being much richer in tone, it is produced by glazing and fresh touches of transparent colour, whereas the tints of Hals seem to have been mixed in the first instance on his palette; hence that undisturbed dexterity of handling which gives so much the appearance of life in his best works. The distinctive characteristics between a portrait painter and a historical painter, is "that the one paints man in general, the other a particular man;" hence, to ennoble the work, it is necessary to make it conform, as much as can be done with safety to the likeness, to the great principles that guide the highest branches of the art – that is, by softening down those features that overstep the boundary of general nature, and assisting those parts that fall short, or are defective. Therefore, when Lawrence painted Mrs. Siddons, the Duke of Wellington, or Lord Brougham, he chose a front view of the face, that their peculiarities might not be too apparent. Now Sir Joshua carried these generalizing principles to so great an extent at times that his sitters did not recognise the striking likeness that some people look for as paramount to all other considerations, which made his pupil, Northcote, remark that there was a class of sitters who would not be content "unless the house-dog barked at it as a sign of recognition." Rembrandt, on the contrary, did not generalize enough; therefore, many portraits were left on his hands, as it is said they were left on Reynolds's. But see the result, those very pictures from the easel of both painters bring higher prices than the more favoured of their likenesses, from being intrinsically fine works of art. The number of portraits Rembrandt painted of himself is a proof of the little encouragement he received in painting the portraits of others. From Sir Joshua's hand we have but two or three, while from Rembrandt's we have nearly fifty. Yet, with all the deficiencies in the art of making up a beautiful face, Rembrandt frequently produced portraits of great feminine beauty: witness "The Lady with the Fan," in the collection of the Marquis of Westminster, and "The Lady," in the Royal Collection. Had he got the same models of female beauty that Titian and Reynolds had, he would, in all probability, have transferred them to the canvas with the same truth and intenseness of feeling that guided his pencil in other matters. Rembrandt's style was that which would have suited Oliver Cromwell, who, when he sat for his portrait, made it a *sine qua non* that the painter should leave out neither warts nor wrinkles. The same truth and verisimilitude that regulated his forms, guided his eye with respect to colour. In his earlier pictures, such as "The Ship Builder," in the Royal Collection, there is a greater degree of hardness and solidity of pigment than in his later works, which possess more the suppleness of flesh. This is also to be observed in the later works of Titian, Velasquez, and Reynolds, and in the later works of our Scottish Velasquez – Raeburn. The portraits of Gainsborough possess this in a high degree. What has been said with regard to Rembrandt laying on his colours with the palette-knife, is very much exaggerated. Many of his heads are as smooth as Reynolds's, and finished with great delicacy and precision; in fact, the versatility of his genius, and the wonderful command over his materials, from indefatigable practice, have given both his pictures and prints that character of having been done in the best style suited to accomplish his object. I have mentioned that Titian keeps his backgrounds often dark, for the purpose of giving a delicacy to his strong shadows in the face; both Vandyke and Rembrandt do this by making the colour of the background amalgamate with the colour of the hair, or dark shades of the head. Rubens, Reynolds, and Lawrence often used a red curtain in contact with their flesh, to produce the same result. The luminous character of the head is certainly better preserved by its giving out rays or similarity of tone to the surrounding background. It has been remarked that the luminous and transparent character of the flesh is enhanced, as in several of Vandyke's portraits, by bringing it in contact with an earthy, dull tint. Vandyke, indeed, when his ground would not permit him, introduced over the shoulders of his females a scarf of this colour. Rembrandt often plunges from the dark shadows of his head into his ground, and thus gives both a breadth and unity. This practice, where the shadows of the face are produced by the same colour as the contiguous background, is certainly the foundation of simplicity.

I think the money value of Rembrandt's portraits may be taken as a criterion of their intrinsic worth as works of art; other masters' decline in producing high prices, Rembrandt's increase – witness the portrait sold the other day at the Duke of Buckingham's, at Stowe; – though the half-length of a burgomaster whom few people ever heard of, it realized seven hundred guineas and upwards. No nameless portrait by Reynolds, under the same disadvantages, would produce an equivalent sum. Sir Joshua's portraits are either branches of our aristocracy, or celebrated public characters. As a knowledge of art advances, works fall naturally into their proper stations. When Reynolds's sister asked Sir Joshua the reason that we never see any of the portraits by Jervas now, he replied, "Because, my dear, they are all up in the garret." Yet this man drove his chariot and four, and received the praises of Pope in verse. Sir Godfrey Kneller would sometimes receive a sum of money and a couple of portraits by Vandyke as payment; but now, a single portrait of the great founder of the Dutch school would outweigh in true value a large number of Kneller's collected talent: yet Rembrandt died insolvent, and Sir Godfrey accumulated a large fortune. And such will be the fate of those who paint for posterity, "and look beyond the ignorant present." The true statement of this change, which of necessity takes place, is, that the man of genius paints according to the high impulse that has been given him, as paramount to every other consideration; the other panders to the caprice and ignorance of those who employ him. This it was that made Reynolds's master, Hudson, exclaim, after Sir Joshua's return from Italy, "Why, Joshua, you don't paint so well as you did before you went abroad!" When men of genius and high talent fall upon favourable times, the result is the reverse, and the fine arts are esteemed, and their professors rewarded according to their excellence. The age in which Titian lived was famous for literary men, who had made the republic of Venice known and honoured through the whole of Italy. The praises of Michelangelo bestowed on the works of the great Venetian, had adorned the name of Titian with a halo of supernatural brightness; so much so, that whilst painting the portrait of the Emperor Charles the Fifth, happening to drop one of his pencils, Charles stooped and picked it up, observing, "that a genius like Titian deserved to be waited on by emperors." Of Reynolds we know that all the beauty and talent of the land flocked to his painting-room, conscious of being handed down to posterity with all the advantages that pictorial science could achieve. The grace of Coreggio was grafted by this great master on the strong stem of Rembrandt's colouring. In opposition to those advantages, we have to remark that the people with whom Rembrandt came in contact were not only of an inferior character, when measured by the standard of grace and dignity, but the troubles of the times militated in a high degree against that encouragement so necessary to the perfection of the art. In spite of these inauspicious circumstances, the genius of Rembrandt has produced works fraught with the highest principles of colour and pictorial effect, and to his want of encouragement in the department of mere common portraiture, we are indebted for many of the most pictorial and splendid specimens of strong individual character in familiar life.

Of all the works by Rembrandt, perhaps no picture has attracted so much attention and observation as his "Night Watch," now in the Museum of Amsterdam. As its dimensions are thirteen feet by fourteen, it secures attention by its size; its effect, also, is striking in a high degree, though Reynolds, in his "Tour to Holland and Flanders," says it disappointed him, having heard so much respecting it. He remarks that it had more of the appearance of Ferdinand Bol, from a prevalence of a yellow, sickly colour. On the other hand, Wilkie says, "Had it been a subject such as 'The Christ before Pilate,' which he has etched, it would have been his finest and grandest work." Though painted in 1642, it possesses all the force and high principles of colour to be found in his later works. Nothing can exceed the firmness and truth of the two figures advancing to the spectator – especially the officer in the light dress – it is modelled with all the force of nature, and the background figures being steeped in the deepest hues of subdued colour, give a strength and richness which nothing can surpass. Of course, there is a want of interest in the story, which is merely an assemblage of the Militia of Amsterdam, on occasion of the expected visit of the Prince of Orange and the daughter of Charles the First, whom he had espoused. The principal pictures by other great masters receive a greater notoriety from the interest of the subject – such as "The Transfiguration," by Raffaelle; "The Peter Martyr," by Titian; "The Miracle of St. Mark," by Tintoretto; "The Martyrdom of St. George," by Paul Veronese; and "The St. Jerome," by Coreggio. Nevertheless, "The Night Watch," by Rembrandt, may safely be classed with the choicest productions of the great painters of Italy and Venice. When we consider that his pictures extend to upwards of six hundred and fifty, the reader will appreciate the difficulty I have felt in describing the peculiar merit which has so indelibly stamped most of them with the passport to posterity.

LANDSCAPES

The landscapes by Rembrandt, unhappily few in number, possess the strong mark of truth for which his works are so strikingly fascinating. They are chiefly small, the largest not exceeding three feet. One of his best is in the collection of the Marquis of Lansdowne, representing a mill seen under the influence of an uncertain twilight; the warm light of the western sky sheds its lustre on the sails of the mill, which stands on high ground; but the other portions of the picture are of dark half-tint, except a reflection of the light on the water towards the foreground. It was exhibited in the British Gallery, in 1815, and attracted great attention. Another picture peculiar to the genius of Rembrandt is in the collection of Sir Richard Colt Hoare, Bart.; it represents a night scene on the skirts of a wood, with a group of figures seated round a fire, the red gleam of which is reflected in a stream that flows along the foreground. A few cattle are partially seen in the obscure portions of the picture, with a peasant passing with a lantern. Other smaller works are in the collections of Sir Robert Peel, Samuel Rogers, Esq., Sir Abraham Hume, and the Marquis of Hertford. His largest picture of this class was formerly in the Louvre, and is now in the public gallery at Hesse-Cassel. In the landscapes of Rembrandt we meet with the same breadth, and hues of a deep tone, without being black or heavy; they are also painted with a full pencil, and rich juicy vehicle. Rembrandt, like Titian, Rubens, and others who were historical painters, seizes upon the great characteristics of nature without entering into the painful fidelity of topographical littleness; the same generalizing principles pervade every variety of subject. Fuseli, speaking of portrait painting as mere likenesses, adds – "To portrait painting thus circumstanced, we subjoin, as the last branch of uninteresting subjects, that kind of landscape which is entirely occupied with the tame delineation of a given spot – an enumeration of hill and dale, clumps of trees, shrubs, water, meadows, cottages, and houses – what is commonly called views. These, if not assisted by nature, dictated by taste, or chosen for character, may delight the owner of the acres they enclose, the inhabitants of the spot, perhaps the antiquary or the traveller, but to any other eye, they are little more than topography. The landscape of Titian, of Mola, of Salvator, of the Poussins, Claude, Rubens, Elsheimer, Rembrandt, and Wilson, spurns all relation with this kind of map-work. To them nature disclosed her bosom in the varied light of rising, meridian, and setting suns – in twilight, night, and dawn."

DRAWINGS BY REMBRANDT

In looking over the numerous portfolios of drawings in public and private libraries, we are struck with the accumulated mass of mediocre talent. Many of them are often well composed, and even well drawn, but they are completely destitute of what constitutes true merit – they possess no distinguishing mark whereby we can discern one master from another; they are struck off with wonderful dexterity, as far as the eye or hand is concerned, but the mind is totally wanting; neither do they possess the peculiar features of natural truth, whose lines are filled with variety, sometimes sharp, sometimes round – in parts faint and delicate, and in other places strong and cutting. On the other hand, when the drawings of great painters are examined, the master mind shines forth in every touch, and we recognise the works of Michelangelo, Raffaelle, Coreggio, and others, at a glance. The drawings of Rembrandt possess this quality in a superlative degree, and the slightest indication seems sufficient to mark the character and leading features of the object represented. His drawings are generally in pen outline, with a wash of bistre, or other warm colour; sometimes he makes use of black and red chalk; they are seldom finished with colours, but have often portions rendered lighter and broader by means of a wash of white. From his great practice in using the point in etching, he not only gives the greatest precision and certainty, but his outline assumes the gentlest delicacy or overpowering boldness.

Everything from his hand seems to possess a largeness of form, and the greatest breadth of light and shade that can be given; this it is that gives them the stamp of truth, so that it is difficult to distinguish between those drawn immediately from nature, and such as are emanations from his imagination. On looking into the catalogue of his effects, we perceive large folios of his drawings, which, though at the sale they produced but small sums, are now marked with their true value. I may notice here a small drawing of "The Death of the Virgin," that brought, at the sale of the late Baron Verstolk, one hundred and sixty guineas. One cannot but regret that the excellent collection of the drawings by Rembrandt and other masters, selected by the late Sir Thomas Lawrence, with great taste and at large sums, should have been lost to the country, though offered in his will at comparatively a small price. Nevertheless, we possess several fine specimens in the British Museum Print-room.

THE ETCHINGS OF REMBRANDT

No painter has gained so much celebrity by his etchings as Rembrandt, both on account of their number and excellence. Claude, Parmegiano, Berghem, Paul Potter, Adrian Ostade, and others, have all been dextrous in using the etching point. Rembrandt's performances have all the interest and beauty of finished works; his making use of the dry point, which was unknown before his application of it, gives his etchings that richness and softness peculiar to himself, for the process in the hands of others has never since been attended with the same triumphant success. The etchings consist of three hundred and sixty-five plates, accompanied by two hundred and thirty-seven variations. I can only here give their titles and dates: the amateur is referred to the descriptive catalogues of Gersaint, Daulby, Bartsch, Claussin, and Wilson. The catalogue by the latter gentleman is the one adopted by the British Museum; I have, however, numbered them according to the Catalogue Raisonné of Rembrandt's Works by Smith, who made use of the arrangement of the Chevalier Claussin. I have also marked those that are of the greatest excellence with a star before the number.

Portraits of the Artist.

1. Portrait of Rembrandt when a young man, having frizzly hair.

2. Portrait of Rembrandt with moustaches, and wearing a bonnet put sideways on his head.

3. Portrait of Rembrandt, represented with a falcon on his right hand.

4. Portrait of Rembrandt, with frizzly hair, and the head uncovered; remarkable for thick lips and a large nose. Very rare.

5. Portrait of Rembrandt, seen in nearly a front view, with frizzled hair, and the head uncovered.

6. Portrait of Rembrandt when a young man, wearing a fur cap and a black habit.

7. Portrait of Rembrandt when young, seen in a front view, wearing a slouched hat, and a mantle lined with fur. Dated 1631.

8. Portrait resembling Rembrandt, seen in nearly a front view, with moustaches, short curling beard, and frizzled hair.

9. Portrait of Rembrandt when young, seen in a three-quarter view, with the head uncovered and the hair frizzled.

10. Portrait of Rembrandt, seen in a front view, having an expression of grimace.

11. Portrait of Rembrandt, seen in nearly a front view, with a flat bonnet on the head.

12. Portrait of Rembrandt when young, seen in a three-quarter view, with head uncovered, and the hair frizzled. (Oval.)

13. Portrait of Rembrandt when young, with the mouth a little open, the head uncovered, and the hair frizzled. Dated 1630.

14. Portrait of Rembrandt, seen in a front view, having a fur cap, and a mantle bordered with fur. Dated 1631.

15. Portrait of Rembrandt, seen in a three-quarter view, with the head uncovered, and the hair frizzled; he has on a mantle buttoned in front. Dated 1631.

✳ 130

16. Portrait of Rembrandt, seen in a front view, wearing a fur cap of a round form, and a mantle. Dated 1631.

17. Portrait of Rembrandt, seen in nearly a front view, having on a bonnet of the usual shape, placed sideways on his head, and a kind of scarf round his neck. Dated 1633.

18. Portrait of Rembrandt, seen in a front view, having on a richly-ornamented cap or turban, and an embroidered robe. He holds a drawn sabre in his hand. Dated 1634.

19. Portraits of Rembrandt and his Wife, on one plate. Dated 1636.

20. Portrait of Rembrandt. He has on a mezetin cap, decked with a feather, and a rich mantle. Dated 1638.

*21. Portrait of Rembrandt, seen in a three-quarter view; he has long curling hair and moustaches; a cap of the usual shape covers the head, and a rich mantle the body. The left arm leans on some stone work. Dated 1639.

*22. Portrait of Rembrandt, seen in a front view, wearing a narrow-brimmed hat, and a plain habit open in front; he is seated at a table, holding a crayon in his hand. Dated 1648.

23. Portrait of Rembrandt, seen in a three-quarter view, with long curling hair; he has on a cap with a small feather in front of it, attached by a ribbon; his mantle is fastened in front by a clasp. Dated 1634. (Oval) (This is the cut plate of the celebrated sabre print.)

24. Portrait of Rembrandt, seen in nearly a front view, having on a fur cap, which covers his forehead to the eyebrows; his curling hair falls on his shoulders, and his robe is bordered with fur. Dated 1630.

25. Portrait of Rembrandt, with the left side of the face strongly shadowed; his frizzled hair falls on the shoulders, and his habit is a little open in front, and lined with fur. Dated 1631.

26. Portrait strongly resembling Rembrandt, seen in a front view, having short frizzled hair, and the mouth a little compressed; he has on a

cap, and wears a mantle attached by a little ribbon.

27. Portrait of Rembrandt, closely resembling No. 1. The face is seen in a front view, and the body in a three-quarter position; the hair is frizzled, and a toupée is on the left side; the eyes and forehead are in shadow.

28. Portrait of Rembrandt, seen in a three-quarter view, with a small beard and mustacheos; a cap of the usual shape covers his frizzled hair, and the dress is composed of a mantle bordered with fur. This is placed by Bartsch and Gersaint among the fancy portraits.

29. Portrait resembling Rembrandt when young, seen in a front view, with round face, large nose, the mouth a little open, short frizzled hair, and a cap on the head; his mantle is attached by four buttons in front. Dated 1630.

30. Portrait of Rembrandt (styled by some writers, "Titus, the Son of the Artist.") It represents a young man, with ragged frizzled hair falling on the shoulders. He is dressed in a habit with a collar. Dated 1639.

31. Portrait of Rembrandt, or very like him, when a young man; he has frizzled hair, and wears a fur cap. (Octagon.) This is inserted by other writers among the fancy heads.

32. Portrait closely resembling Rembrandt, seen in a front view, with a cap on; the attitude is that of a person drawing. Engraved very lightly, and almost without shadow, on a narrow plate.

33. Portrait closely resembling Rembrandt, seen in a front view, having on a cap of the usual shape, the top of which is cut off by the edge of the plate. Dated 1630. These figures are ill formed.

Subjects from the *Old Testament*.

34. Adam and Eve in Paradise; the latter has the forbidden fruit in her hand, which she has received from the tempter, who is seen in the form of a serpent in a tree, with an apple in his mouth. Dated 1638.

*35. Abraham entertaining the three angels at the door of his house.

Dated 1656.

36. Abraham offering up his Son. Dated 1655.

37. Abraham sending away Hagar and Ishmael. Dated 1637.

38. Abraham caressing his son Isaac.

39. Abraham with his son Isaac. The subject represents the moment when the son asks his father, "Where is the sacrifice?" Dated 1645.

40. Four Subjects to illustrate a Spanish Book. These were originally engraved on one plate, which was afterwards cut into four. They represent as follows: –

Jacob's Dream on the plain of Padan Aran. Four angels are ascending and descending the ladder. Dated 1655.

David preparing his Sling to attack Goliath. Dated 1655.

The Image seen by Nebuchadnezzar in his Dream. Dated 1655.

The vision of Ezekiel. Dated 1655.

41. Joseph relating his Dream to his Parents, in the presence of his Brethren. Dated 1638.

42. Jacob lamenting the supposed Death of his Son Joseph.

43. Joseph and Potiphar's Wife. Dated 1634.

*44. The Triumph of Mordecai.

45. David on his knees in prayer. Dated 1652.

46. Blind Tobit leaning on a Staff, followed by his Dog. Dated 1651.

47. The Angel departing from Tobit and his Family. Dated 1641.

*48. The Angel appearing to the Shepherds, and announcing the Birth of the Saviour. Dated 1634.

49. The Nativity of the Saviour.

*50. The Adoration of the Shepherds.

51. The Circumcision. Dated 1654.

52. The Circumcision, differently composed.

53. The Presentation in the Temple.

54. The Presentation in the Temple, differently composed.

55. The Presentation in the Temple, differing from the preceding. Dated 1630.

56. The Flight into Egypt. Dated 1633.

57. The Flight into Egypt, differently composed. No date.

58. The Flight into Egypt, differing from the preceding.

59. The Flight into Egypt, differing from the preceding. Dated 1651.

60. The Flight into Egypt, differing from the preceding.

61. A *Reposo* of the Holy Family by night.

62. A *Reposo* of the Holy Family. Dated 1645.

63. A *Reposo* of the Holy Family, supposed to be unique.

*64. The Return from Jerusalem of the Holy Family. Dated 1654.

65. The Virgin, with the Infant Jesus in the Clouds. Dated 1641.

66. The Holy Family.

67. The Holy Family, differently composed. Dated 1654.

68. Jesus amidst the Doctors. Dated 1654.

69. Jesus disputing with the Doctors. Dated 1652.

70. Jesus amidst the Doctors, differently composed. Dated 1636.

*71. Christ preaching to the People.

72. The Tribute Money.

73. Christ driving the Money Changers out of the Temple. Dated 1635.

74. Christ with the Woman of Samaria. The third proof is dated 1658.

75. Christ with the Woman of Samaria, differently composed. Dated 1634.

*76. The Resurrection of Lazarus; styled the Little. Dated 1642.

77. The Resurrection of Lazarus; styled the Great. No date.

*78. Christ Healing the Sick. This beautiful print is known under the appellation of "The Hundred Guilder Print." No date.

*79. Christ in the Garden of Olives. Dated 165. The last figure is wanting.

80. Christ before the People. Dated 1655.

81. Christ on the Cross between the two Thieves, styled "The Three Crosses." Dated 1653.

*82. The *Ecce Homo*. Dated 1636.

*83. The Descent from the Cross. Dated 1633.

84. Christ on the Cross between the two Thieves.

85. Christ on the Cross.

86. The Descent from the Cross. Dated 1642.

*87. The Descent from the Cross; a night piece. Dated 1654.

*88. The Entombment.

89. The Virgin lamenting the Death of the Saviour.

90. Christ in the Tomb.

*91. Christ at the Table with the two Disciples of Emmaus. Dated 1654.

92. Christ at the Table with the two Disciples of Emmaus. Dated 1634.

93. Christ in the midst of his Disciples, and the incredulity of St. Thomas. Dated 1650.

94. The Good Samaritan. Dated 1633.

95. The Return of the Prodigal Son. Dated 1636.

96. The Decollation of St. John. Dated 1640.

97. Peter and John at the Beautiful Gate of the Temple. Dated 1659.

98. Peter and John at the Gate of the Temple, differently composed.

99. St. Peter on his Knees, with a Key in either hand. Dated 1645.

100. The Martyrdom of St. Stephen. Dated 1635.

101. The Baptism of the Eunuch. Dated 1641.

*102. The Death of the Virgin. Dated 1639.

Saints.

103. St. Jerome seated at the foot of a tree. Dated 1634.

104. St. Jerome at his devotions. Dated 1632.

105. St. Jerome at his devotions, with a lion behind him. Dated 1634, or 1635.

106. St. Jerome seated, with spectacles on, writing. Dated 1648.

107. St. Jerome seated, reading in a large book held with both hands.

108. St. Jerome seated at a table in a room. Dated 1642.

109. St. Jerome on his knees, meditating before a skull.

110. St. Francis on his knees at his devotions, with a crucifix and a book before him. Dated 1657.

Historical, Allegorical and Fancy Subjects.

111. A Youth surprised by the Apparition of Death. Dated 1639.

112. An Allegorical subject, allusive to the demolition of a statue offensive to the Low Countries. Dated 1659.

113. Fortune Reversed, an allegorical subject, allusive to some hero upon whom Fortune has turned her back. Dated 1633.

*114. The Marriage of Jason and Creusa. Dated 1648.

115. The Star of the Kings, an ancient Dutch custom on the feast of the kings.

116. A Lion Hunt; several huntsmen on horseback attacking a lion. Dated 1641.

117. A Lion Hunt, differently composed to the preceding.

118. A Lion Hunt, also differing from the above.

119. A Battle. The subject represents a group of horsemen advancing, full speed, with swords, javelins, &c.

120. Three Figures in Oriental dresses, accompanied by a dog. Dated 1641.

121. The Blind Bagpiper amusing some cottagers.

122. The Spanish Gipsy.

123. The Rat Killer. Dated 1632.

124. The Rat Killer, differently composed.

125. The Goldsmith.

126. The Pancake Woman. Dated 1635.

127. The Game of Kolf. Dated 1654.

128. The Jews' Synagogue. Dated 1648.

129. The Schoolmaster. Dated 1641.

130. The Mountebank. Dated 1635.

131. The Draughtsman.

132. A Peasant with his Wife and Child.

133. A Jew wearing a high Cap. Dated 1639.

134. The Onion Woman. Dated 1631.

135. The Peasant with his hands behind him. Dated 1631.

136. The Card Players. Dated 1641.

137. The Blind Fiddler. Dated 1631.

138. A Man on Horseback.

139. The Polander, with his hands united.

140. The Polander, with his sword and staff.

141. The Polander, with a cane in his left hand. Dated 1631.

142. An old Man, standing with his back to the spectator.

143. A Peasant Man and a Woman walking together.

144. A Philosopher seated, with a pen in his hand.

145. A Man seated at a table, on which is an open book.

146. An old Man seated, resting his arm on a book.

147. An old Man without a beard. Dated 1631.

148. An old Man with a short beard, leaning on a staff.

149. An old Man with a long beard, in the dress of a Persian. Dated 1631.

150. The Blind Jew, standing with his back to the spectator, leaning on a staff.

151. Two Figures in Venetian Dresses.

152. A Doctor feeling the Pulse of a Patient.

153. The Skater.

*154. The Hog with his Legs tied. Dated 1643.

155. A little Dog lying asleep.

156. A Shell, known under the appellation of "The Damier." Dated 1650.

Beggars.

157. A Beggar seated, with his hands united.

158. A Beggar and his Wife.

159. A Beggar standing, resting both hands on a staff.

160. A Beggar standing, holding a stick in his right hand.

161. A Beggar Man and a Woman, standing in conversation. Dated 1630.

162. A Beggar Man and a Woman by the side of a Bank.

163. A Beggar with a Stick in his right Hand. In the manner of Callot.

164. A Beggar in a slashed Cloak. Dated 1631.

165. A Beggar Woman, with a calebash hanging behind her.

166. A Beggar, wearing a fur cap, and resting both hands on a staff.

167. An old Beggar Woman asking Charity. Dated 1646.

168. Lazarus Klap, or the Dumb Beggar. Dated 1631.

169. A Beggar with a wooden Leg, standing with his hands behind him.

170. A Beggar sitting at the side of a Wall.

171. A Beggar sitting on a Bank. Dated 1630.

172. A Beggar sitting, with his Dog by his side. Dated 1651.

*173. Three Beggars at the Door of a House. Dated 1648.

174. A Beggar with one Hand in the Breast of his Jacket, in a cold day. Dated 1634.

175. A Beggar with his Hands behind him.

176. A Beggar with a wooden Leg, and a stick in his hand.

177. A Peasant with his Hands behind him, and a basket at his feet.

178. A Peasant Woman with a Bottle attached to her Waist.

179. A Beggar. This is merely a sketch.

180. A Beggar Man and a Woman walking side by side.

181. A Beggar wrapped up in his Mantle.

182. A Sick Beggar lying on the ground.

Academical Subjects.

183. The French Bed. Dated 1646.

184. The Friar among the Corn.

185. The Flute Player and the Shepherdess. Dated 1642.

186. An old Man sleeping, and a couple caressing.

187. A pot-bellied Man, with a pack at his back, and a pouch by his side. Dated 1630.

188. A Woman crouching under a Tree. Dated 1631.

189. A Painter drawing after a Model.

190. A naked Man, seated. Dated 1646.

191. Academical Figures of Men.

192. The Bathers. Dated 1631.

193. A Man sitting naked for a Model. Dated 1646.

194. A Woman sitting before a Dutch Stove.

195. A Woman sitting naked on a Bank.

196. A Woman at the Bath. Dated 1658.

197. A Woman sitting naked with her feet in the water. Dated 1558.

198. Venus in the Bath. She is seated at the foot of a tree, with her feet in the stream.

*199. A Naked Woman sitting on a Bed, with an arrow in her hand. Dated 1661.

200. Antiope, Jupiter, and a Satyr. Dated 1659.

201. A Woman lying asleep on a Couch. A Satyr in the background.

202. A Negress lying on a Couch. Dated 1658.

Landscapes.

203. A Landscape, in which is introduced a cow.

204. A Landscape, distinguished by a large tree growing by the side of a house.

205. A Landscape, with a bridge, styled "Six's Bridge." Dated 1645.

206. A View of Omval, near Amsterdam. Dated 1645.

*207. A View of Amsterdam.

208. A Landscape, with a huntsman on a road, followed by two dogs.

*209. A Landscape, known under the appellation of "The Three Trees." Dated 1643.

*210. A Landscape, distinguished by a man carrying a yoke of pails.

211. A Landscape, with a canal, on the banks of which are two houses embosomed in trees. Washed in bistre, or India ink.

212. A Landscape; the scene is remarkable for a coach passing along a road in the centre of the view.

213. A Landscape, with a terrace, and a road over it in the centre.

*214. A Landscape, with a village situate near the high road. Dated 1650.

215. A View of the village of Randorp, remarkable for an old tower, of a square form. Dated 1650.

216. A Landscape, in the foreground of which may be noticed a man seated, drawing.

217. A Landscape, with a pond, on the bank of which sits a woman with a child in her lap; a shepherd stands behind her. Dated 1644.

218. A View in Holland. Some cottages among trees are seen in the centre, and a canal flows along the front.

219. A Landscape, representing a woody scene, with a vista on the right. Dated 1652.

220. A Landscape, with an old tower rising above the roofs of some houses.

*221. A Landscape distinguished by a road leading to a village, on which is a shepherd with a flock of sheep. Dated 1636.

222. A Landscape, with a cottage and barn. Dated 1641.

223. A Landscape, with a large tree and a cottage on the left, and divided obliquely by a canal. Dated 1641.

224. A Landscape, remarkable for an obelisk standing on the left, and a village stretching along the distance.

225. A Landscape, with three houses on the left, backed by trees, and near these is a woman followed by a dog; on the opposite side is a canal, with a sailing vessel on it.

226. A Landscape, with a cluster of trees at the side of a road; a second road divides the scene in the centre.

227. A Landscape, with a cottage on the left, and in the centre an alley of trees; close to the front is a man with a stick on his shoulder.

228. A Landscape, with a large piece of water. The name and date are inscribed at the foot of the trunk of a tree on the right. Dated 1645.

229. A Landscape, with a cottage near the middle, on either side of which is a tree, and in front an enclosure of paling.

*230. A View, supposed to be that of the house in which the artist was born, and the adjacent windmill. Dated 1641.

231. The Gold-weigher's Field. The scene is remarkable for a mansion placed near the centre, and a wood stretching along the left of it; on the right is seen the steeple of a church rising above some trees. Dated 1651.

232. A Landscape, distinguished by a canal, on which are two swans. Dated 1650.

*233. A Landscape, with a canal, and a boat lying alongside the shore. Dated 1650.

234. A Landscape, with a canal in front, at which a cow is drinking.

235. A View of a Village, remarkable for an old square tower. Dated 1653.

236. A Landscape, with a river on the left, on which is seen the half of a boat.

237. A Landscape, in which may be noticed a little man, and in the distance two windmills and a steeple.

238. A Landscape of an upright form, having a large tree in the middle, and a man and a woman in front.

239. A Landscape, with a farm-house partly concealed by trees, and surrounded by a wood fence.

240. A Landscape, with a river, on which are two sailing boats, and on the left of the print is seen a man seated on a barge, angling.

241. A Landscape, traversed obliquely by a canal, on the bank of which sits a man, angling.

242. A Landscape, distinguished by a low house built on the bank of a canal, and above the roof of which rises the gable of a second house; near these are some trees and a boarded fence.

243. A Landscape, in which may be noticed a house of two stories high, a windmill, and a river with a sailing boat on it.

244. A Landscape, divided by a canal; in the centre rises a large tree, near which is a cottage partly concealed by trees. Dated 1659.

245. A Landscape, with a barn filled with hay, adjacent to which is a cottage with a fence in front of it, and a clump of trees.

246. A Landscape, with a canal in front, and a boat on it; the scene is further distinguished by a large cottage, with the upper part of the door open.

247. A Landscape, with a large house on the right, constructed of wood, and having three chimneys; beyond this object are two hovels surrounded by trees, at the foot of which flows a river.

248. A Landscape, on the left of which may be noticed a peasant drawing water from a well, behind which grows a lofty tree. A dray-cart is also introduced.

249. A Landscape. This scene is distinguished by a château with eight pointed towers. This is doubted by M. de Claussin.

250. A Landscape, with several trees in the distance, in addition to which may be noticed a large trunk of a tree, and in front of it is a bull attached by a cord.

251. A Village Scene. The view represents, on the right, two houses with pointed roofs; above which rises a round tower.

252. This view exhibits a portion of a village, with six thatched houses, only one of which is shadowed and finished. Dated 1659.

253. A Landscape, with a large canal extending throughout the scene, on the banks of which are two men angling.

Portraits of Men.

254. Portrait of a Man, seen in nearly a front view, with his left hand resting on a table. Dated 1642.

255. Portrait of a young Man, seated, with his right hand placed on his thigh, and the left on his breast. Dated 1650.

256. Portrait of an old Man. He is in the act of raising the right hand to his bonnet.

257. Portrait of an old Man, seen in nearly a front view. He appears to be seated, and his attention is directed downwards.

258. Portrait of a Man, with long straight hair covered with a cap; a chain is suspended round his neck, to which is attached a cross. Dated 1641.

259. An old Man with a long beard, having on a fur cap, and a large mantle, sitting in an arm-chair.

260. A man with a short beard, represented in a front view, with a fur cap on his head, and dressed in an embroidered mantle. Dated 1631.

261. Portrait of Jan Antonides Vander Linden. He wears a handsome robe, and is represented in a garden, with a book in his hand.

262. An old Man, with a square-shaped beard, a fur cap on his head, and the right hand placed on his belt. Dated 1640.

*263. Portrait of Janus Silvius. He is represented in nearly a front view, dressed in a robe bordered with fur, a ruff, and a cap, and seated at a table, with one hand placed on the other. Dated 1633.

264. An old Man with a long beard, seated at a table, with both hands on a book.

265. A young Man seated at a table, on which are some books. He has on a cap, and wears a robe lined with fur. Dated 1637.

266. Portrait of Manasseh Ben Israel. He is distinguished by a pointed beard, and is seen in a front view, having on a broad-brimmed hat, and a large collar. Dated 1636.

*267. Portrait of Dr. Faustus. This person is represented in a profile view, having on a white cap and a robe, standing, with one hand on a table, and the other on his chair.

268. Portrait of Renier Hanslo. He is seen in a front view, seated at a table, on which is placed a large open book. Dated 1641.

269. Portrait of Clement de Jonge, a print dealer. He is seated in nearly a front view, wearing a slouched hat, a mantle, and a small collar; he wears gloves, and the right hand is placed in front. Dated 1642.

270. Portrait of Abraham France, an amateur of prints. He is seated in an arm-chair examining a print which he holds in his right hand.

*271. Portrait of the elder Haaring. He is represented in a front view, seated, resting both arms on the elbows of his chair, and the fingers of his right appear to hold a pinch of snuff.

*272. Portrait of young Haaring, son of the preceding Burgomaster. He is seen in a front view, apparently seated, with his right hand resting on the elbow of his chair. Dated 1655.

*273. Portrait of young Lutma, a celebrated goldsmith. He is seated, holding in his right hand a metal figure. Upon a table near him are a silver tazza, and other objects relative to his occupation. Dated 1656.

274. Portrait of Jean Asselyn, surnamed Crabatje. He is represented standing in a front view, having on a slouched hat; his body is enveloped in a mantle, and his right hand rests on a table, on which are a palette and several books.

*275. Portrait of Ephraim Bonus, a Jew doctor. He appears to be in the act of descending some stairs, and his right hand is placed on the baluster. His dress consists of a high-crowned hat, and a pendent frill. Dated 1647.

276. Portrait of Utenbogardus, a Dutch minister. He is seen in a front view, seated, holding with his right hand a book, which lies open on a table. (*Oval.*) Dated 1635.

*277. Portrait of Jean Silvius, a learned man and a minister. This print is enclosed in an oval, around which is written, *Spes mea Christus,* &c.

*278. Portrait of Utenbogaerd, known under the appellation of the "Gold Weigher." He is seated, holding a pen in his right hand, which rests on a large book lying open on a table. His attention is directed to a youth, to whom he is giving a bag of money. Dated 1639.

279. Portrait of Coppenol, a celebrated writing master, styled "The Little Coppenol." He is seated at a table, holding a pen in his right hand, which he rests on some paper, and the left is also placed on the same sheet; a boy stands behind him, with his hat in his hand.

*280. Portrait of Coppenol, called "The Great," to distinguish it from the preceding. He is also seated near a table, holding with both hands a sheet of paper, and between the fingers of the right is a pen.

*281. Portrait of Tolling, a Lawyer. He is seen in a front view, seated at a table, on which is a large book, resting both arms on the elbows of his chair, and holding his spectacles in his hand; he has on a slouched hat.

*282. Portrait of the Burgomaster, Jan Six, when twenty-nine years old. He is represented full-length, standing near an open window, engaged in reading a book, which he holds with both hands. This precious work of Rembrandt is dated 1647.

✳ 148

Fancy Heads of Men.

283. A Head of an Asiatic, seen in a front view, having on a calotte. The dress consists of a furred robe, adorned with a gold chain and a medal. Signed, Rembrandt, Venitiis fecit. Dated 1635.

284. A Head of a similar person, seen in a profile view, having on a turban, and a robe bordered with fur. Signed, Rembrandt, Venitiis fecit.

285. A third Head, Asiatic; he has a large beard, and is seen in a profile view, having on a turban, decked in front with a feather. Signed, Rembrandt, Venitiis fecit, 1635.

286. The Bust of a Man, with long hair, and a short frizzled beard, seen in nearly a profile view, having on the usual shaped cap peculiar to the master.

287. The Bust of an old Man, with a long beard, seen in nearly a front view. He has on a fur cap, and wears a mantle, attached in front by clasps.

288. The Bust of an old Man, with a long beard, and a bald head in front; he is seen in a front view, bending a little forward, in such a manner as to throw a shadow over the face.

289. An old Man, seen in a profile view, having a short beard and a bald head. His dress consists of a robe bordered with fur. Dated 1630.

290. The Bust of an old Man without a beard, having a bald head, and seen in a profile view.

291. The Bust of an old Man, seen in a profile view, with a bald head, inclined a little forward. Dated 1630.

292. A small Bust of an old Man, with a bald head, which is bent considerably forward; the face is seen in a three-quarter view.

293. The Bust of an old Man, with a beard and frizzled hair, seen in a three-quarter view. Dated 1631.

294. The Bust of an old Man, with a bald head, which inclines forward, and is turned a little to the right; the mouth is considerably open. Dated 1631.

295. A small Bust of an aged Man without a beard; the face is turned towards the right, and a large fur cap covers the head.

296. The Bust of an elderly Man, with a short frizzled beard. He is seen in a three-quarter view, having on a turned-up cap; the mouth is open, and he appears to be calling to some one.

297. A Head very similar to the preceding, but smaller in size, and extremely rare.

298. A small Bust, the head of which partakes of the character of a Turkish slave. He has on a large high cap, turned up. The body is slightly sketched out.

299. A very small Bust of a Man, similar in character to the preceding; seen in a profile view, having mustacheos. He has on a cap, the upper part of which hangs over, and a frill surrounds the neck.

300. The Bust of a Man, seen in a front view, having on a cap in the shape of a calotte, and a mantle bordered with carmine.

301. The Bust of a Man, with the head uncovered and seen in a front view; his hair is frizzled, and his mouth a little on one side.

302. The Head of an old Man, with a short beard and a bald crown; his neck is enveloped in fur. The shoulders are only slightly indicated.

303. The Bust of a Man, represented in a three-quarter view, with the head bending forward. He has on a fur cap, and a robe bordered with fur, which is open in front, and shows a vest under it. Dated 1631.

304. The Bust of a Man, seen in nearly a profile view, having a pouting mouth, resembling a negro, and a short frizzled beard. He has on a calotte, and a robe bordered with fur, attached in front with a single button.

305. A Bust of an old Man, with a grey beard and bald in front,

represented in a three-quarter view, with the head inclining. He has on a hairy coat with a collar. Dated 1630.

306. A Half-figure of a young Man, represented in a profile view, having short frizzled hair. He wears a large cravat enriched with lace, and a coat with large sleeves and girt with a belt. Dated 164 ; the last figure is omitted.

307. A Bust of a Man, seen in a three-quarter view, having mustacheos. He has on a large hat with a broad brim, a coat buttoned in front, and a pendent frill. Dated 1630.

308. A Bust of an old Man with a large beard, seen in nearly a front view, with a fur cap on.

309. A Bust of an old Man, with a large square-shaped beard, seen in a three-quarter view. He has a cap of the usual shape, and a robe bordered with fur. Dated 1637.

310. A Bust of an old Man, with a similar beard to the last. The face is represented in a three-quarter view, having on a large cap, and a robe bordered with fur.

311. A Bust of an old Man with a pointed beard, seen in a three-quarter view, with a bald front, and the eyes bent downwards; the body is enveloped in a cloak.

312. A Bust of an old Man with a straight beard, seen in a profile view. He has on a small pointed cap. Dated 1631.

313. A Philosopher, with a large square-shaped beard, seen in a profile view, having on a large cap decked with fur; an hour-glass and a skull are faintly introduced. Engraved on wood. This print is doubted by the Chevalier Claussins.

314. An elderly Man, represented in a three-quarter view, apparently seated; he has mustacheos, and a tuft of beard, and wears a large high cap, and a robe bordered with white fur. Dated 1630.

315. A small Bust of a Man, seen in a front view, with the usual shaped cap on his head, and the body enveloped in a mantle. Dated 1631.

✳ 151

316. A Bust of a Man, seen in a profile view, having on a cap with pendent ear straps; the shoulders are covered with a mantle, relieved by a small frill.

317. A Bust of a Man with a bald head, seen in a three-quarter view; the shoulders are covered with a mantle bordered with fur. Dated 1631.

318. A Bust of an old Man, with a very large square-shaped beard, seen in nearly a front view. The head inclines forward, and the eyes are directed downwards. Dated 1630.

319. A very small Head, of a grotesque character, seen in a profile view, having on a fur cap, surrounded by a band.

320. Another small Head, having the appearance of being that of a beggar; the mouth is open, as if he were calling to some one; he has on a pointed cap, and a coat attached by a single button.

321. A Bust of a young Man, the head only of which is finished. He has on a large slouched hat.

322. A Bust of a young Man, with a hat on, of the same form as the preceding.

323. A Bust of a young Man, with a cap on, decked with feathers, and represented at a window. M. Claussins thinks this to be of a doubtful kind.

324. A Bust of a Man, with mustacheos, and frizzled hair, which falls on the right shoulder.

325. A Bust of an old Man, with mustacheos, and a tuft of beard, represented in a three-quarter view, having on a high fur cap, and a fur cloak.

326. A Bust of an old Man, with a long beard, and a bald head in front, seen in a profile view; a robe, bordered with fur, covers his shoulders.

327. A Bust of a Man, with a cap on, decked with feathers. He is seen

in a front view, having a beard and mustacheos, and wearing a frill round the neck.

328. A Bust of an old Man, with a white beard, having on a turned-up cap, and a mantle bordered with fur.

329. A Man, having the appearance of a negro, represented in nearly a profile view. He has on a turban decked with a feather, and holds a cane in the right hand.

Portraits of Women.

*330. Portrait of a Woman, styled, "The great Jewish Bride." She is seated, resting her right hand on the elbow of her chair, and holding a roll of papers in the left.

331. A Head, similar to that of the preceding print, and supposed by some amateurs to have been a study for it, but M. Claussins, in his catalogue, combats that opinion.

*332. Portrait of a Woman, styled, "The little Jewish Bride." Her face is seen in a three-quarter view, and she appears to be standing, with her hands crossed on her waist. Dated 1633.

333. An aged Woman, seated at a table, with her hands placed one on the other; a black veil covers her head, and a mantle, bordered with fur, envelopes her shoulders.

334. An aged Woman; she appears to be also seated, and is seen in a three-quarter view, with a kind of bonnet on her head, and a veil over it; her dress terminates in a frill.

335. Portrait of a young Woman, seen in nearly a profile view, seated near a table, on which is a book; her right hand is concealed by her robe, and the left placed on the book. Dated 1634.

336. An aged Woman meditating over a book. She is seated, having her right hand under her robe, and the left on a book lying on a table. A half-figure, looking to the left.

337. Portrait of a Woman, seen in a profile view. Her hair is tastefully arranged, and decked with pearls; two rows of the same adorn her neck, and the sleeves of her robe are open. Dated 1634.

338. Portrait of an elderly Woman, seen in a profile view. She is seated, with the left hand placed on her breast, and the right on the elbow of her chair. Dated 1631.

339. A Bust Portrait of the Mother of Rembrandt, represented in nearly a front view, with a veil on her head. Her left hand is placed on her breast. Dated 1631.

340. An elderly Woman sleeping. She appears to have been fatigued with reading, and having removed her spectacles from her eyes, has fallen asleep while resting her head on her hand.

341. An aged Woman, resembling the Mother of Rembrandt. She is seen in a three-quarter view, with a linen covering over her head, which falls on her shoulders. Dated 1633.

342. A Head of an elderly Woman, having also the resemblance of Rembrandt's Mother. She is seen in a front view, with the mouth compressed. She has on a cap of the usual form. Dated 1628.

343. A Bust of an elderly Woman, having the same character as the preceding. She is seen in a three-quarter view, with a covering on the head, turned up over the right ear, and falling on the left. Dated 1628.

344. A Bust of the Mother of Rembrandt. She is seen in a front view, with the usual kind of cap on the head, and a robe bordered with fur, which is only slightly sketched in.

345. An old Woman in a black veil. This bust represents the face in a three-quarter view; the veil falls on the shoulders, and her robe is turned up with fur. Dated 1631.

346. A young Woman, represented in nearly a profile view, with a basket on her right arm, and a pouch suspended to the left. She has on a small flat hat, and a tippet over her shoulders.

347. A Bust of a Moorish Woman, seen in nearly a profile view,

having on her head a scarf turned up in front, decked with a feather, and falling behind her head.

348. A Bust of an aged Woman, lightly etched. She is seen in a three-quarter view, with a bonnet on, in the form of a turban, and lappets hanging on either side, and the dress consists of a fur robe.

349. A Bust of a Woman, seen in a three-quarter view, with the head enveloped in a kerchief, the ends of which hang on either side. The body is unfinished.

350. A Head of an elderly Woman, seen in a three-quarter view, with the eyes bent downwards.

351. A Woman seated, resting her head on her hand, and turning over the leaves of a book with the other.

352. An elderly Woman, seen in nearly a profile view, with spectacles on, and holding with both hands a book, which she appears to be reading.

Studies of Heads and Other Objects.

353. A Head of Rembrandt, together with studies of old Men and Women, and other objects, on the same plate.

354. A Study of a Horse, two Heads, a part of a House, and other objects, on the same plate.

355. Rembrandt's Wife, and five other Heads, on the same plate. Dated 1636.

356. Five Heads of Men on one sheet,[1] one of which, placed on the right, wears a square cap, and another, seen on the opposite side, has on a fur cap.

357. Three Heads of Women on one sheet, one of them, occupying the centre and top, is seen in a front view, with one hand raised to her face.

---

1 This plate was afterwards cut into five, and the several heads are arranged in their proper order.

358. Three Heads of Women on one sheet. This print is distinguished by one of the women resting her head on her hand, asleep. Dated 1637.

359. Two Women in separate Beds; several Heads, and studies of an old Man and Woman, with sticks in their hands; on one sheet.

360. A Head of Rembrandt, and other studies, on the same sheet. Dated 1651.

*361. A Study of a Dog, the head only of which is finished.

362. A Sketch of a Tree, and other objects, on the same sheet.

363. Two small Figures, one of which, having on a high crowned cap, is seen to the knees; the form of the other is but imperfectly traced, and the other objects are still more indistinct.

364. Three Heads of old Men on one sheet. They are all seen in a profile view, and placed in the same direction.

365. A Study of a Female Head, very lightly etched. She has on her head a kind of mob cap, and the body is turned to the right.

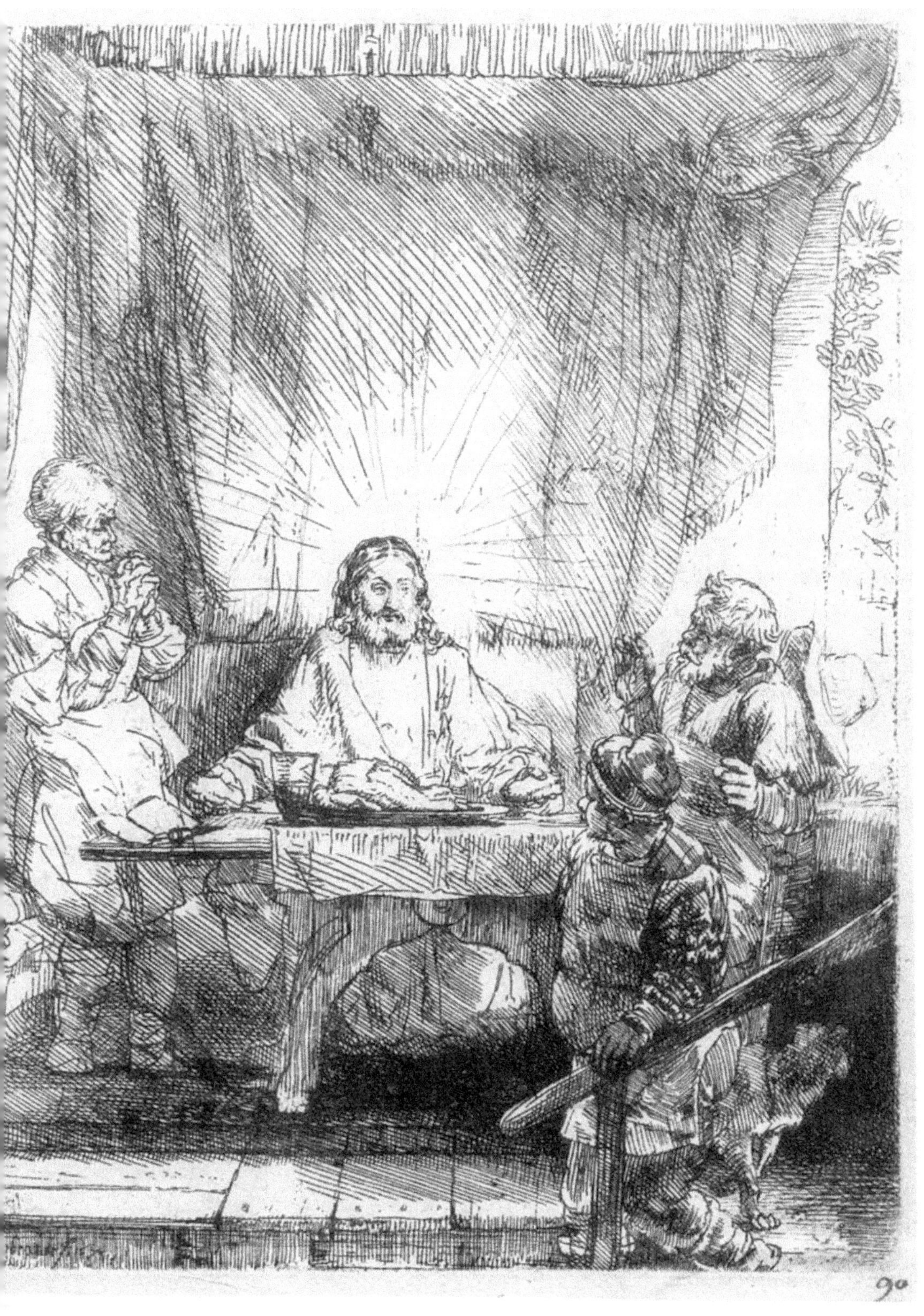

Rembrandt, Christ At Emmaus, 1654

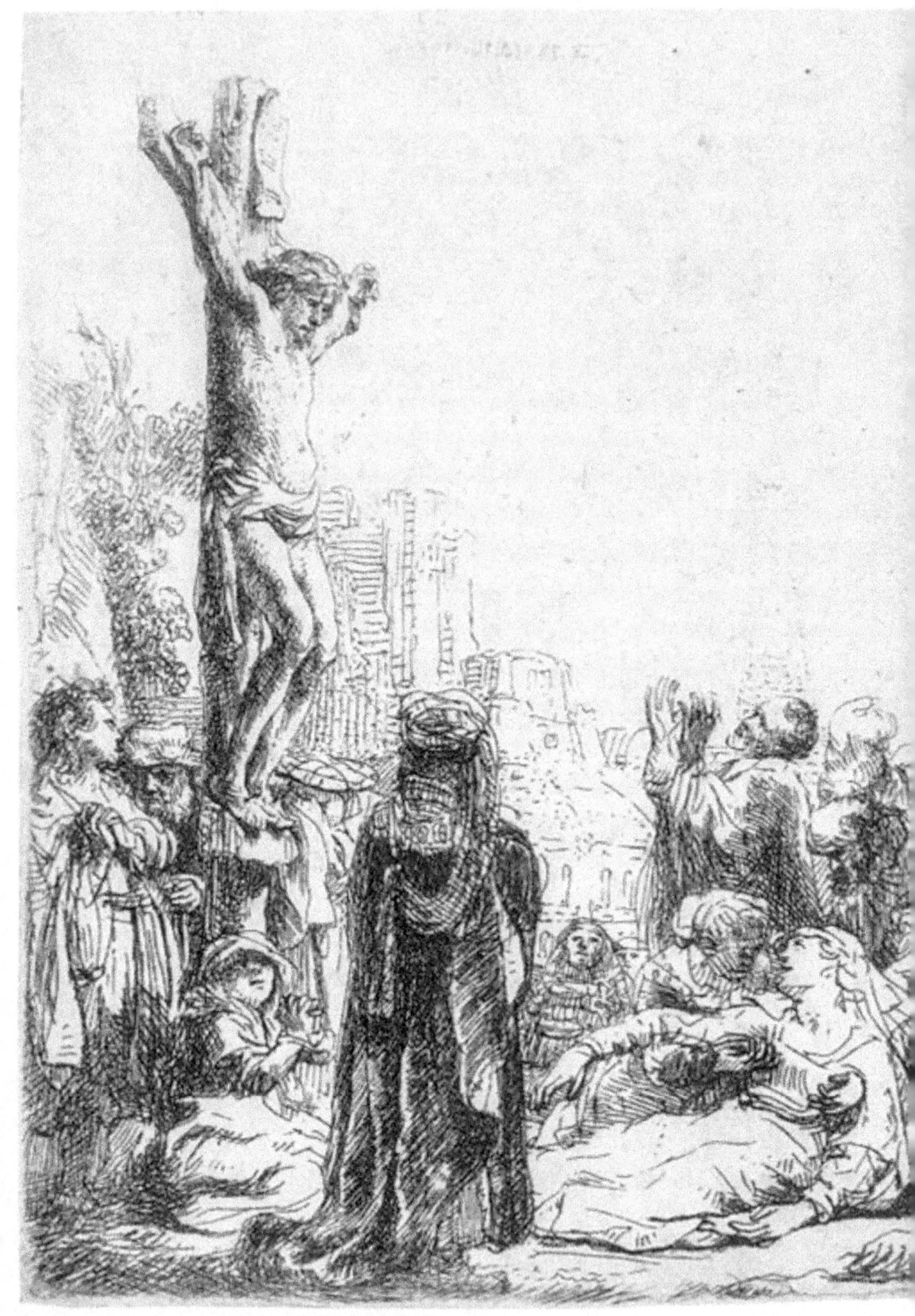

Rembrandt, The Crucifixion, 1637, Vienna

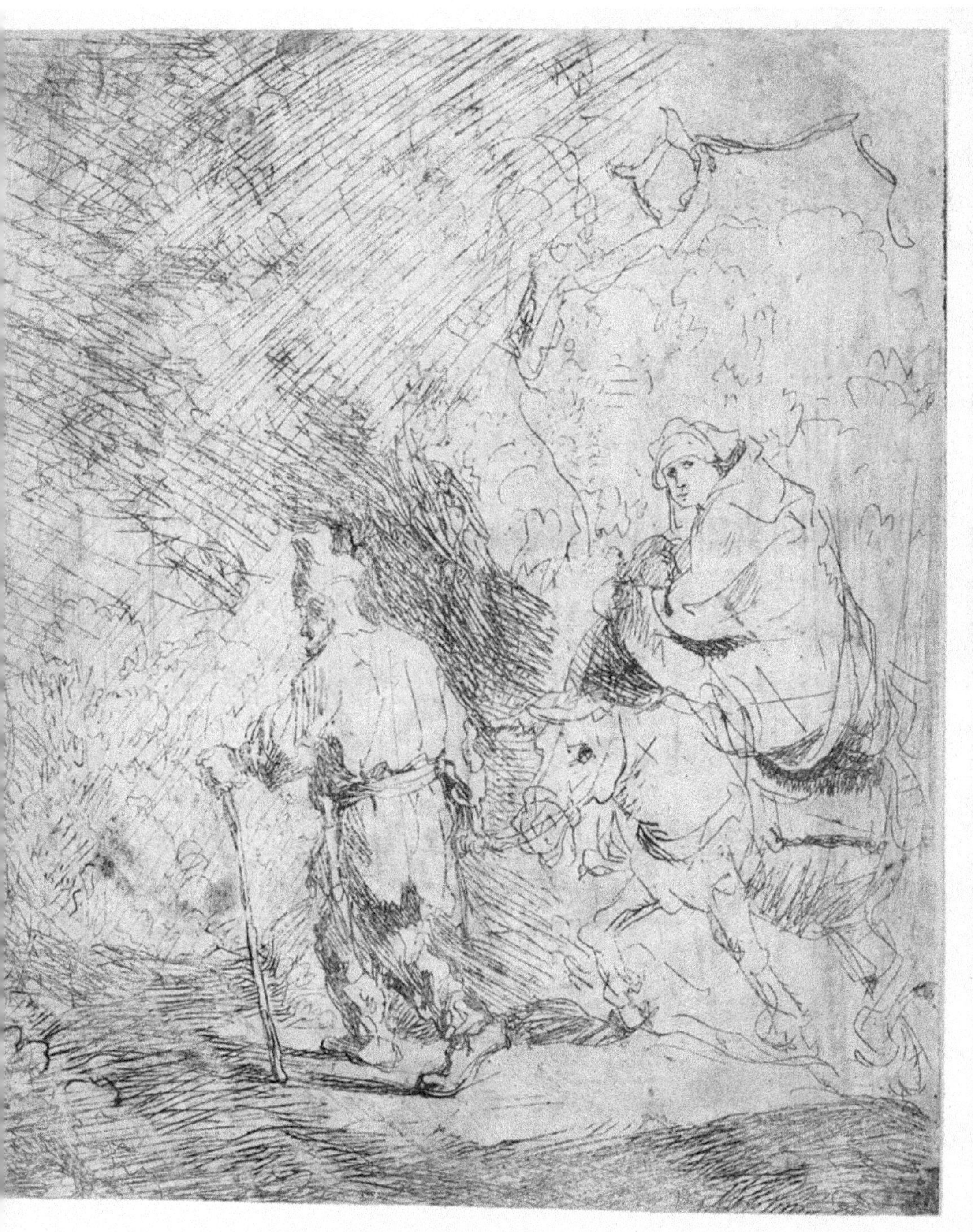

Rembrandt, The Flight Into Egypt, 1627, Rijksmuseum, Amsterdam

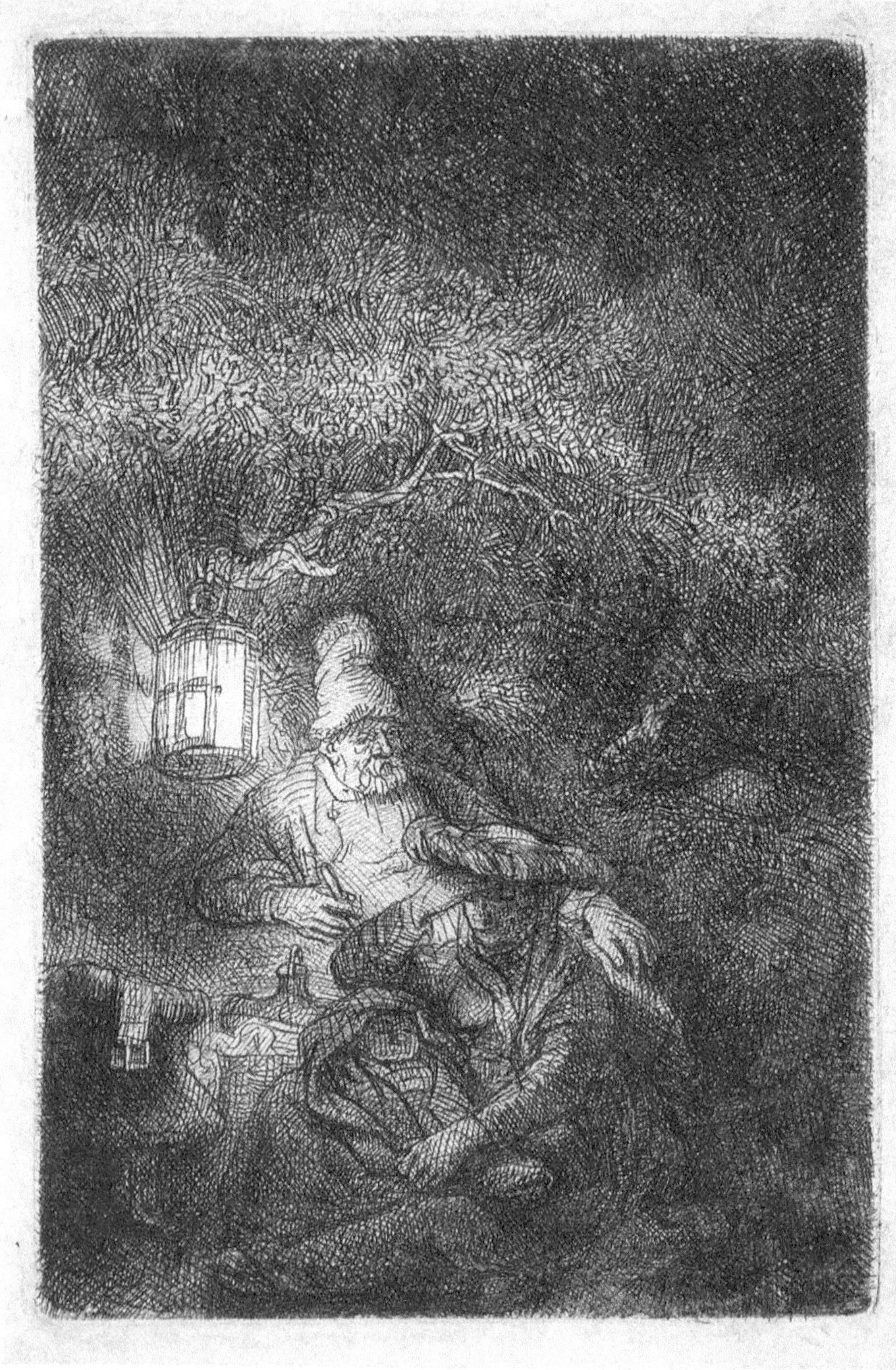

Rembrandt, The Rest on the Flight Into Egypt, Rijksmuseum, Amsterdam

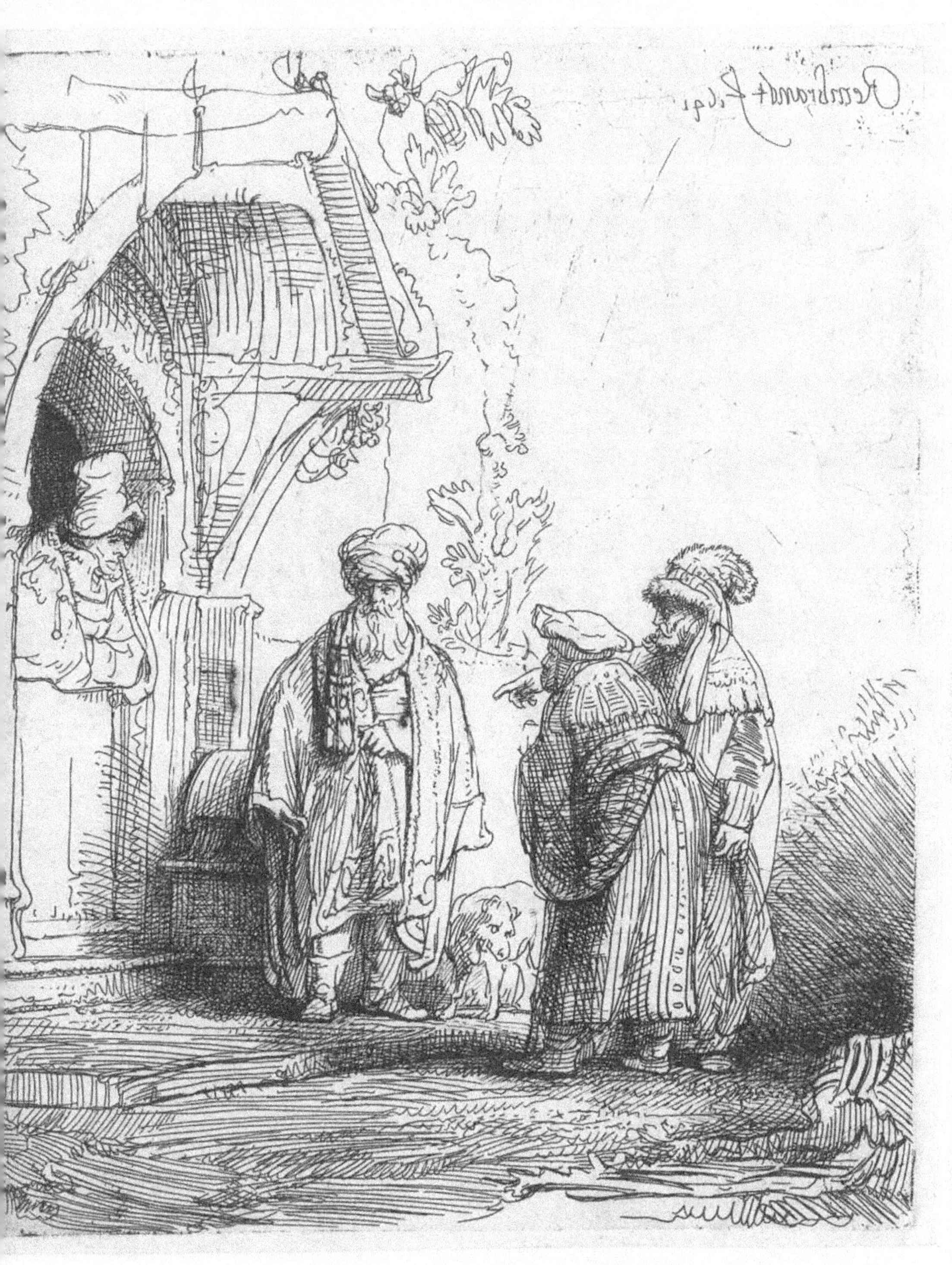

Rembrandt, Jacob and Laban, 1641, Rijksmuseum, Amsterdam

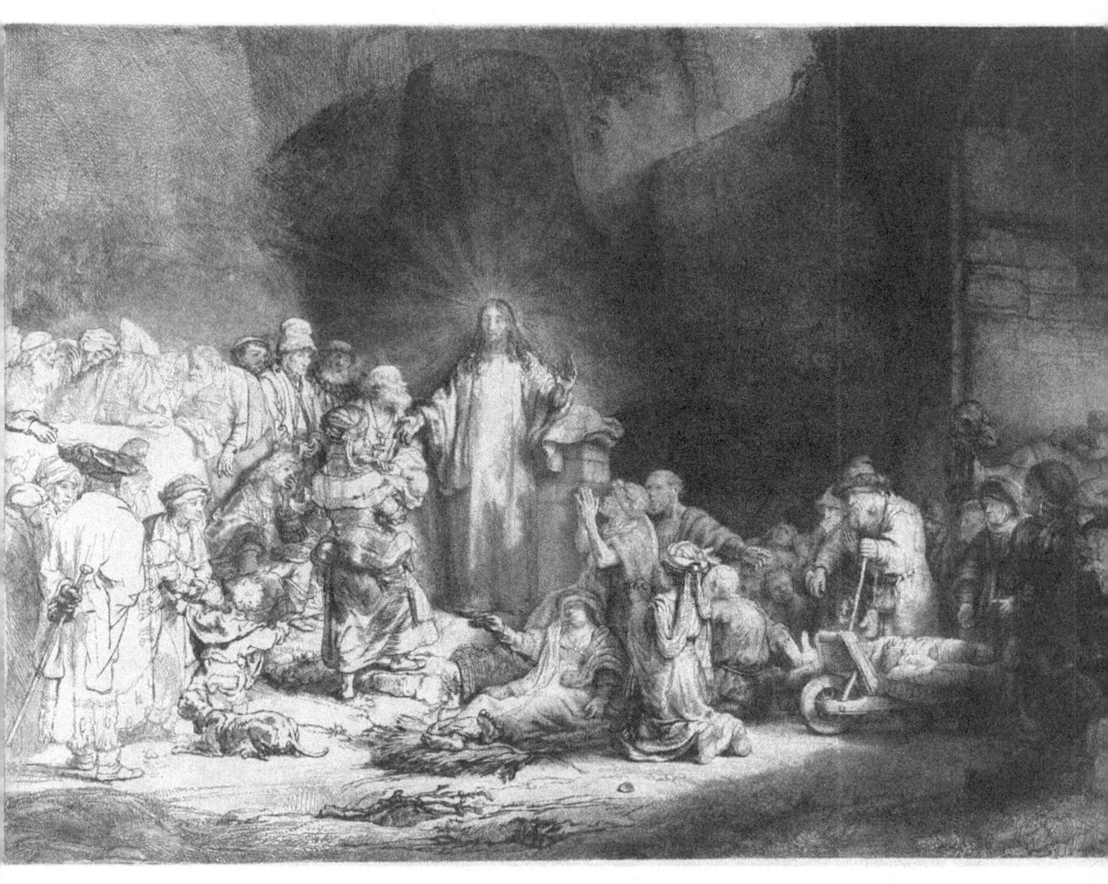

Rembrandt, The Little Children, 1646-50, Rijksmuseum, Amsterdam

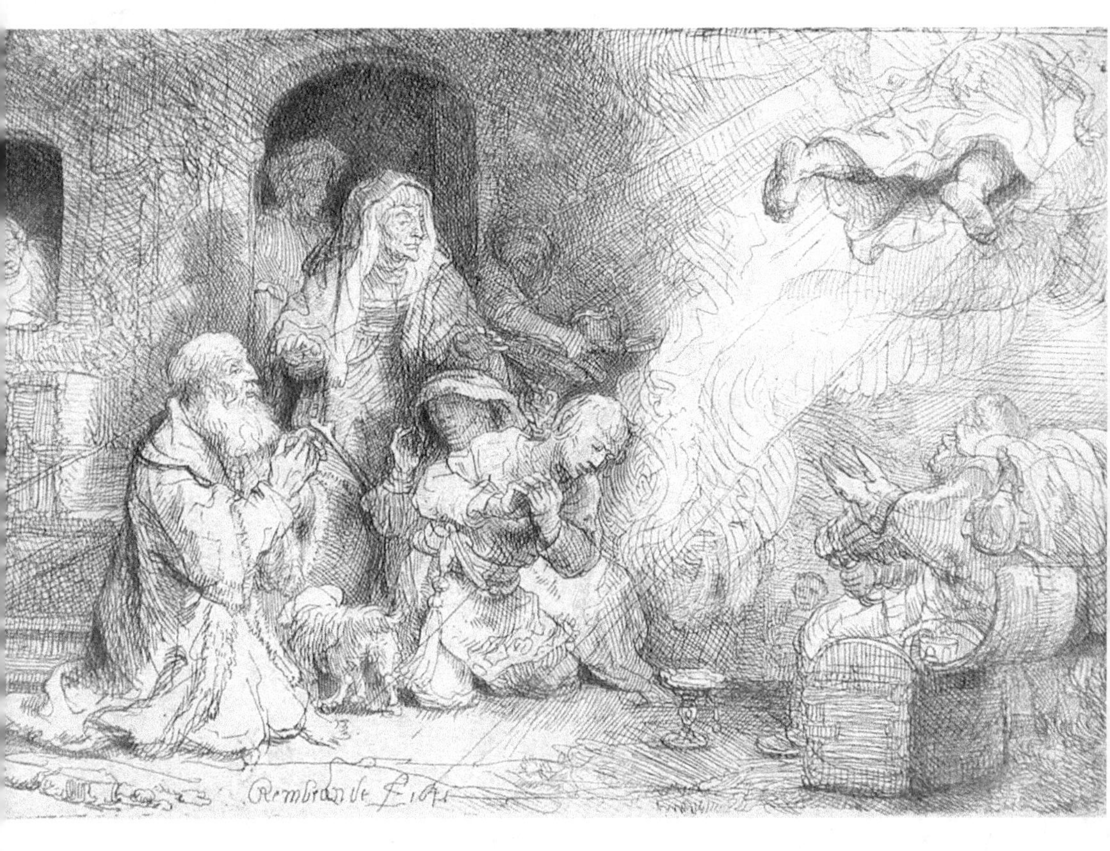

Rembrandt, The Angel Departing From the Family of Tobit, Los Angeles

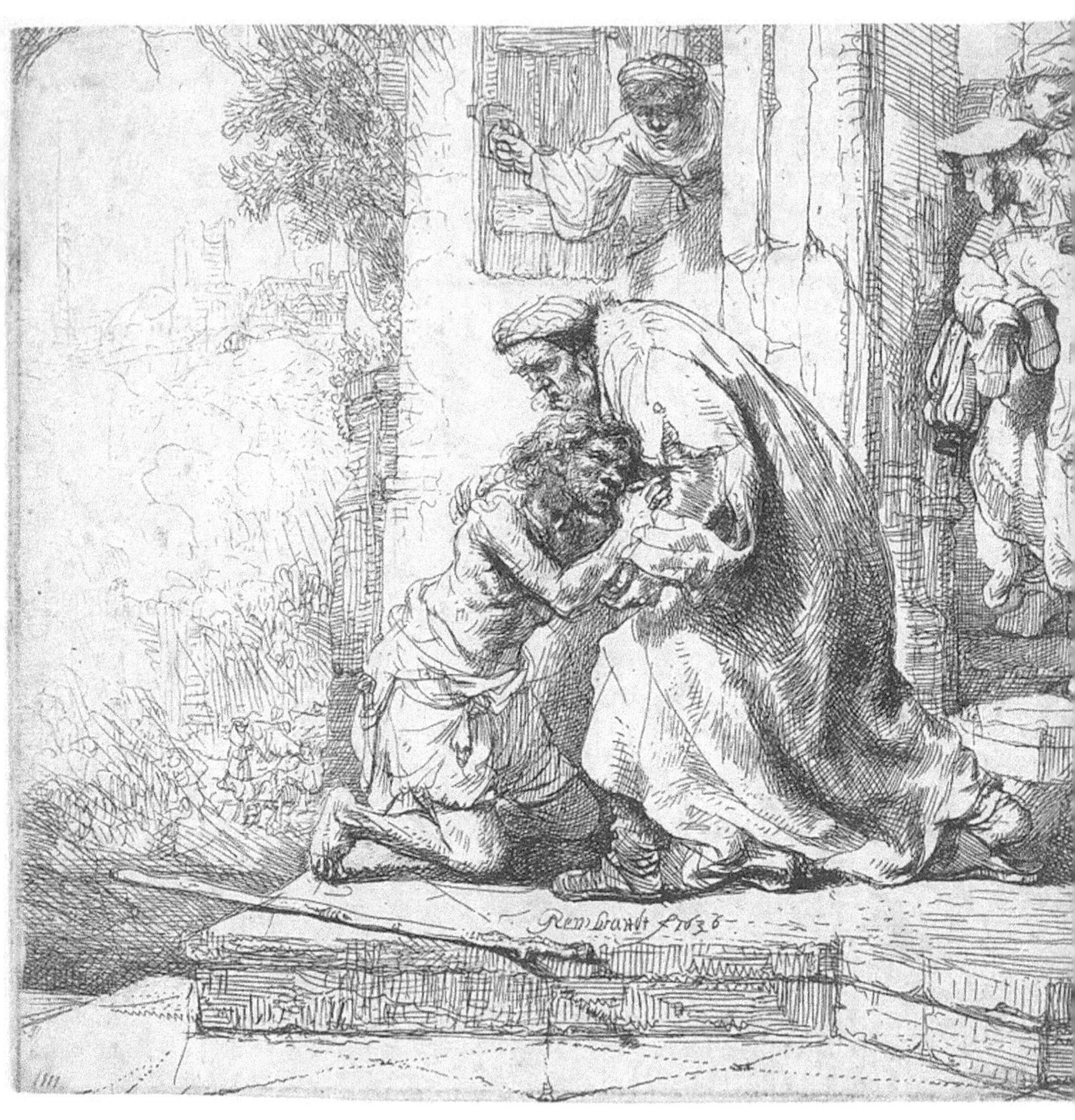

Rembrandt, The Return of the Prodigal Son, 1636, Rijksmuseum, Amsterdam

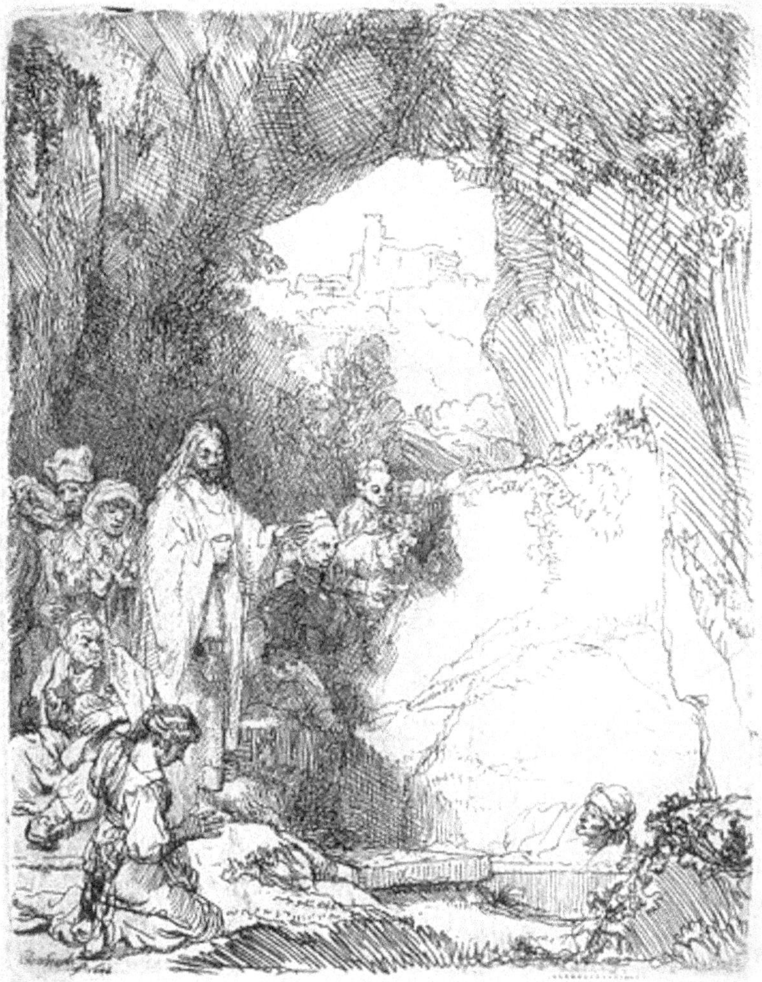

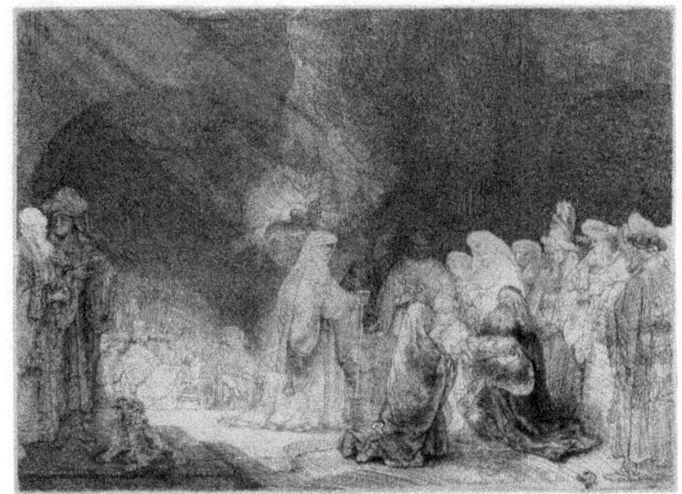

Rembrandt,
The Raising of Lazarus, 1642,
Rijksmuseum,
Amsterdam (above).
The Presentation In the
Temple, 1639,
British Museum (Right).

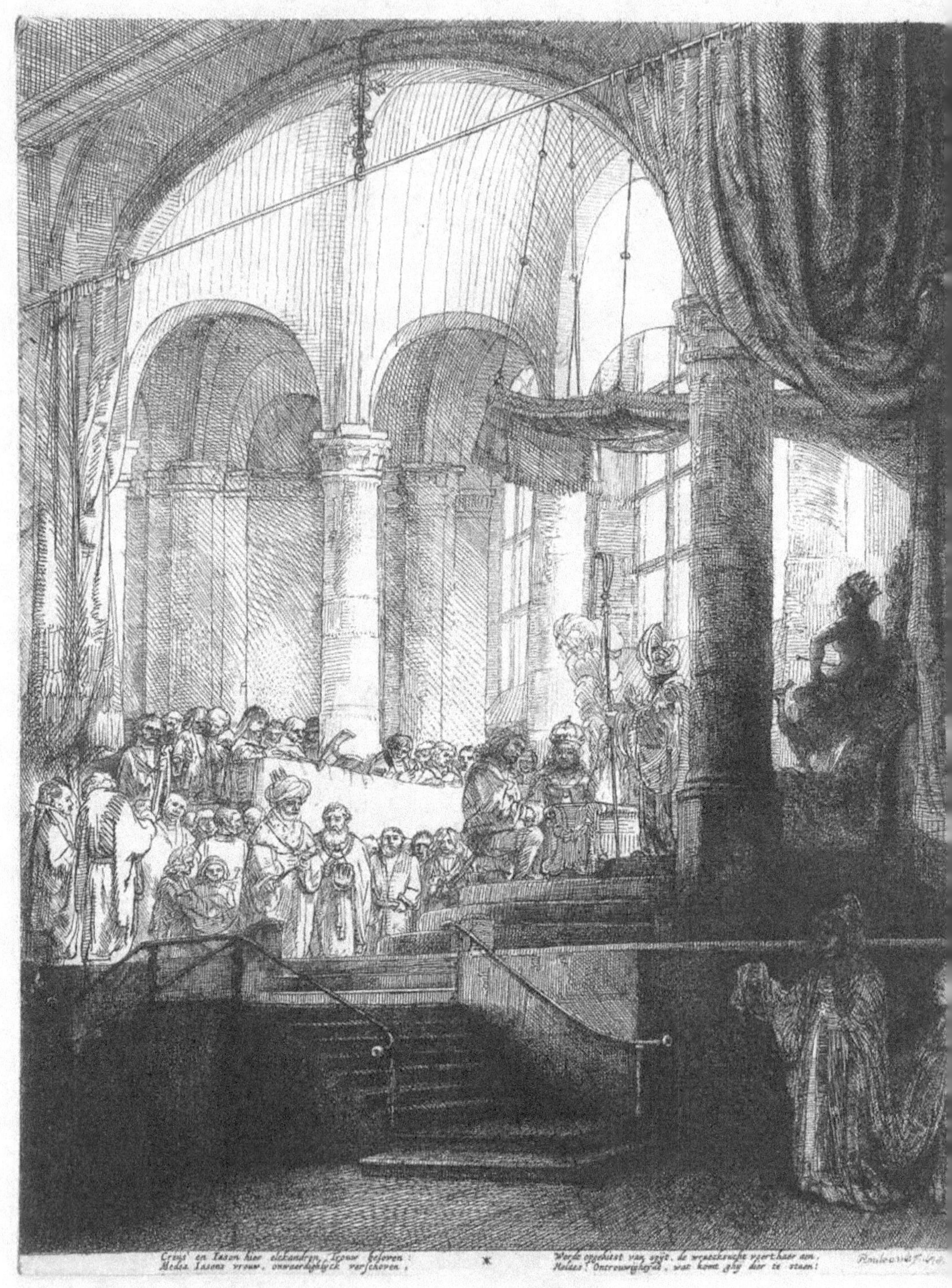

Rembrandt, Medea, 1648, Rijksmuseum, Amsterdam

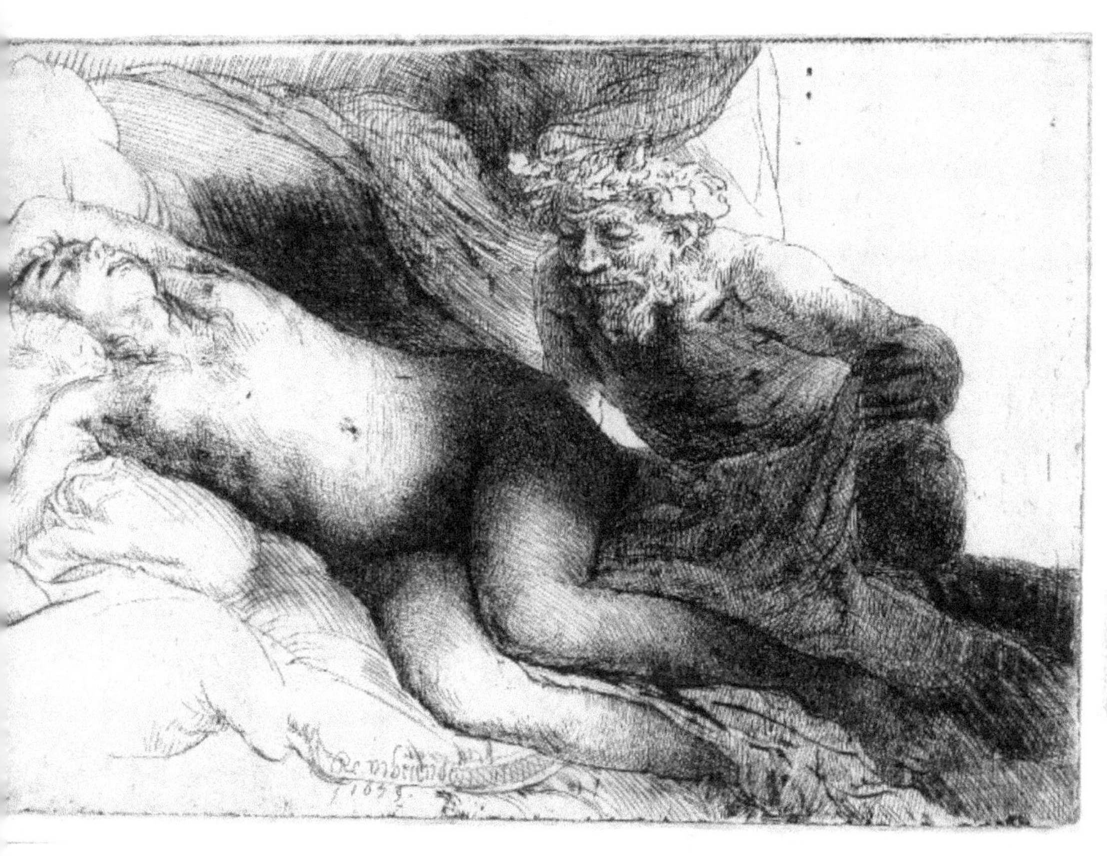

Rembrandt, Jupiter and Antiope, 1659, British Museum

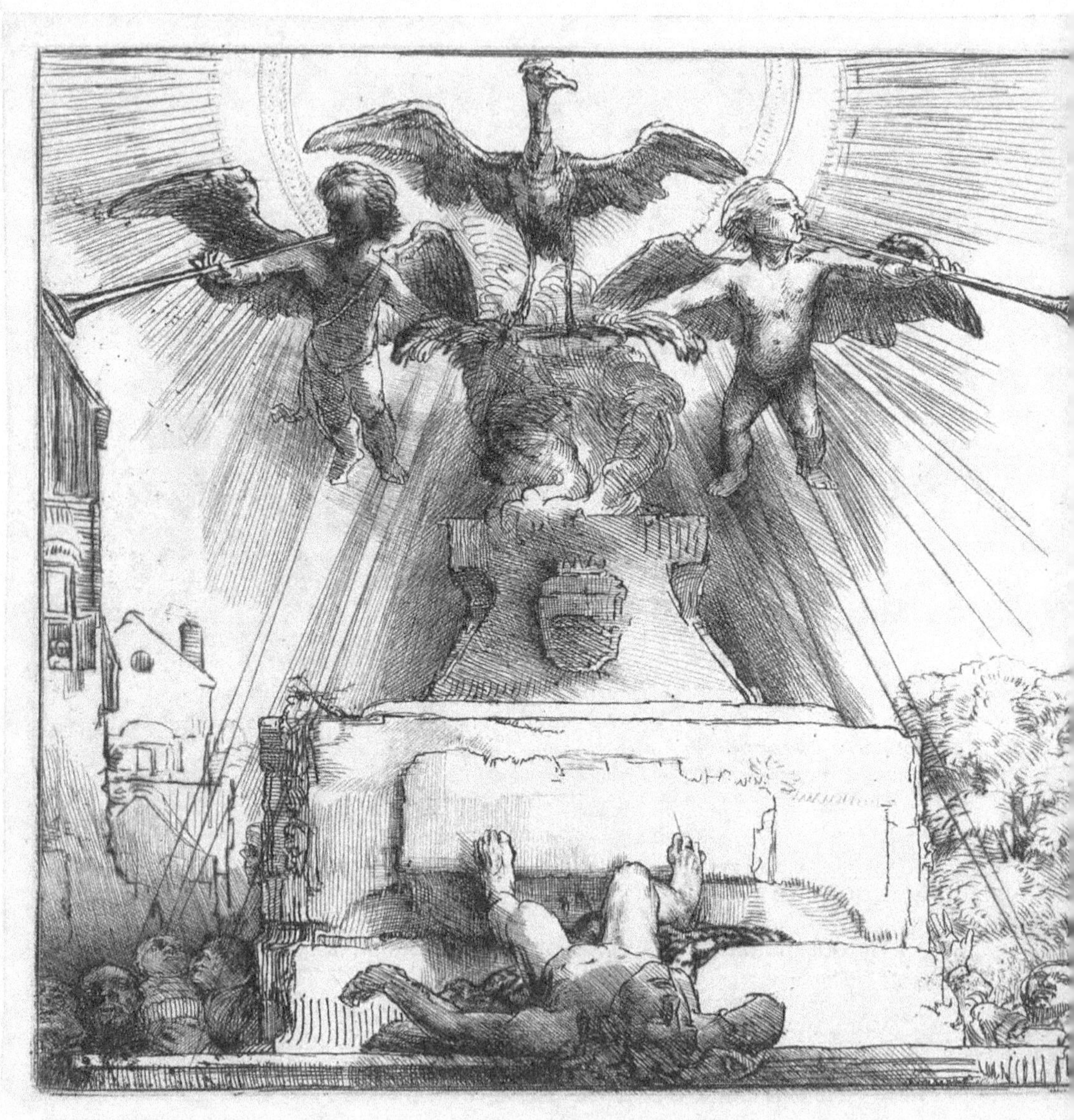

Rembrandt, The Phoenix, or the Statue Overthrown, 1658

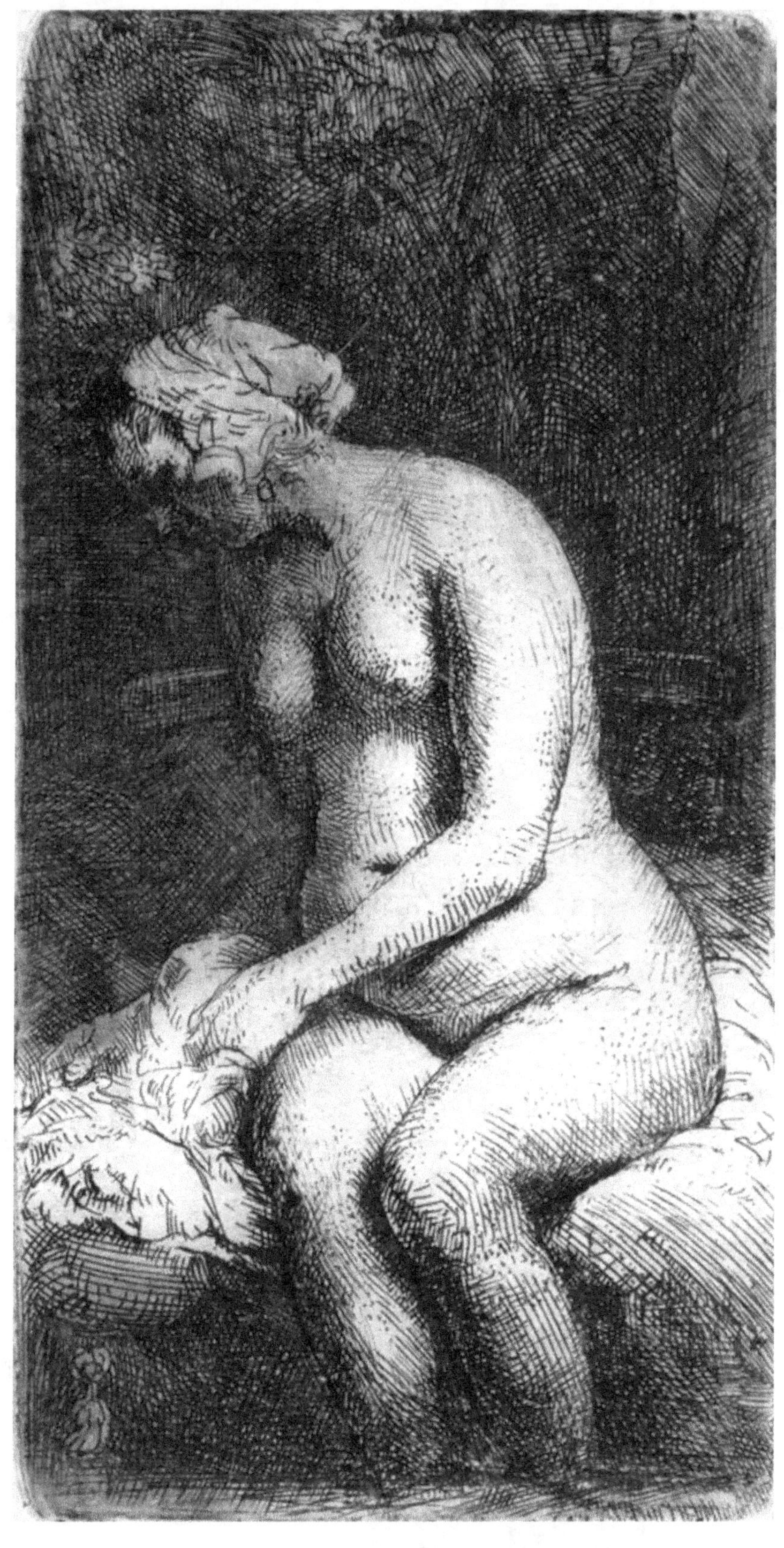

Rembrandt, Seated Nude, 1658

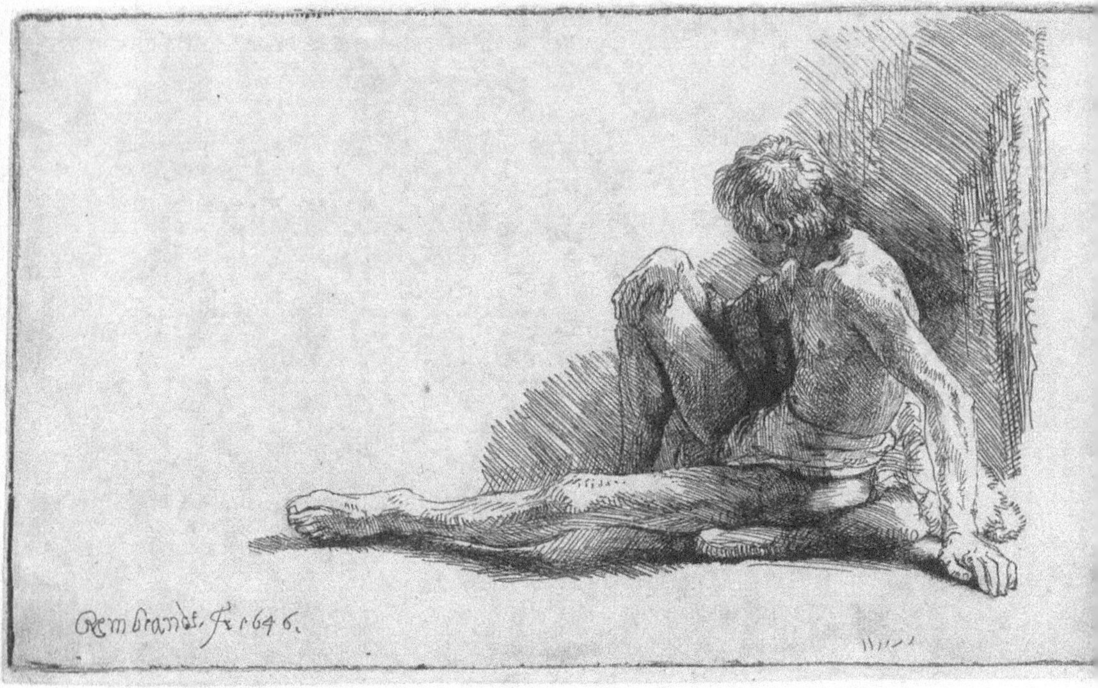

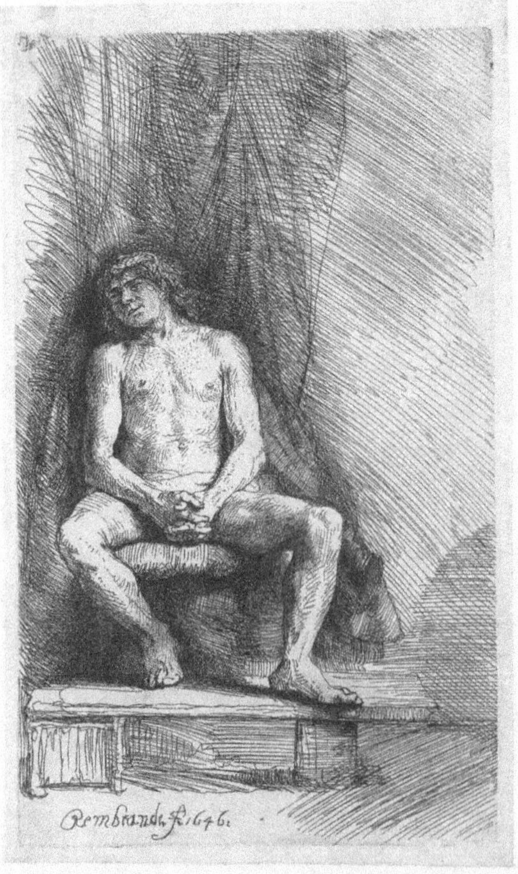

Rembrandt, Nude Man Seated,
1646 (above).
Nude Man Seated Before a Curtain,
Rijksmuseum, Amsterdam (left).

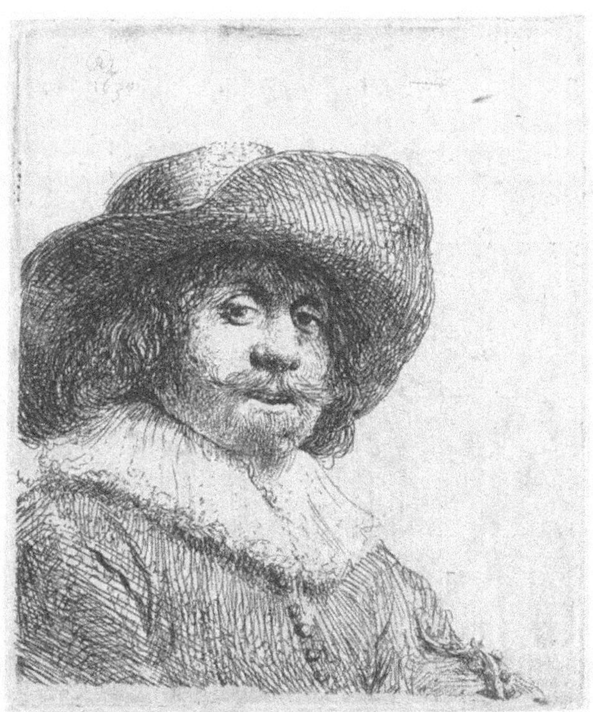

Rembrandt, Man In a Broad-rimmed Hat, 1638 (above).
Man At a Desk, 1641 (below). Both Rijksmuseum, Amsterdam.

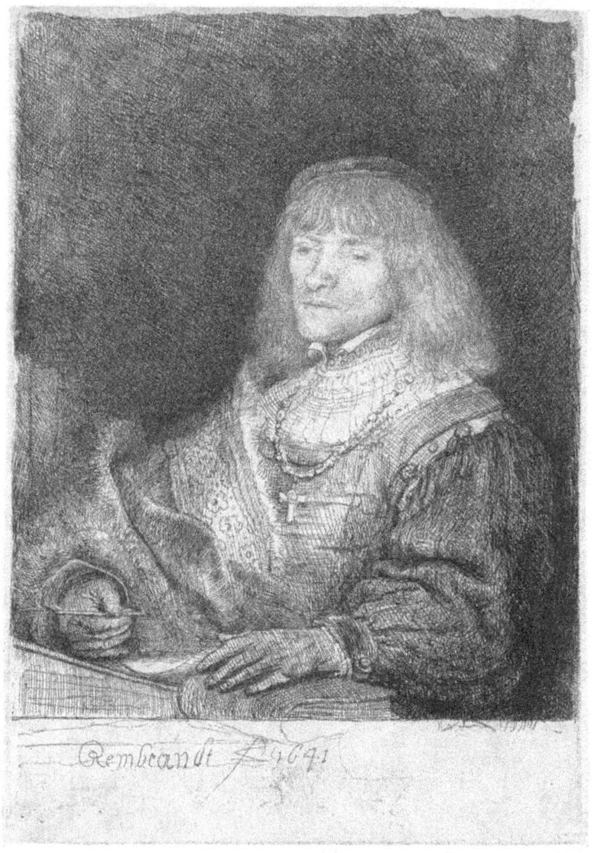

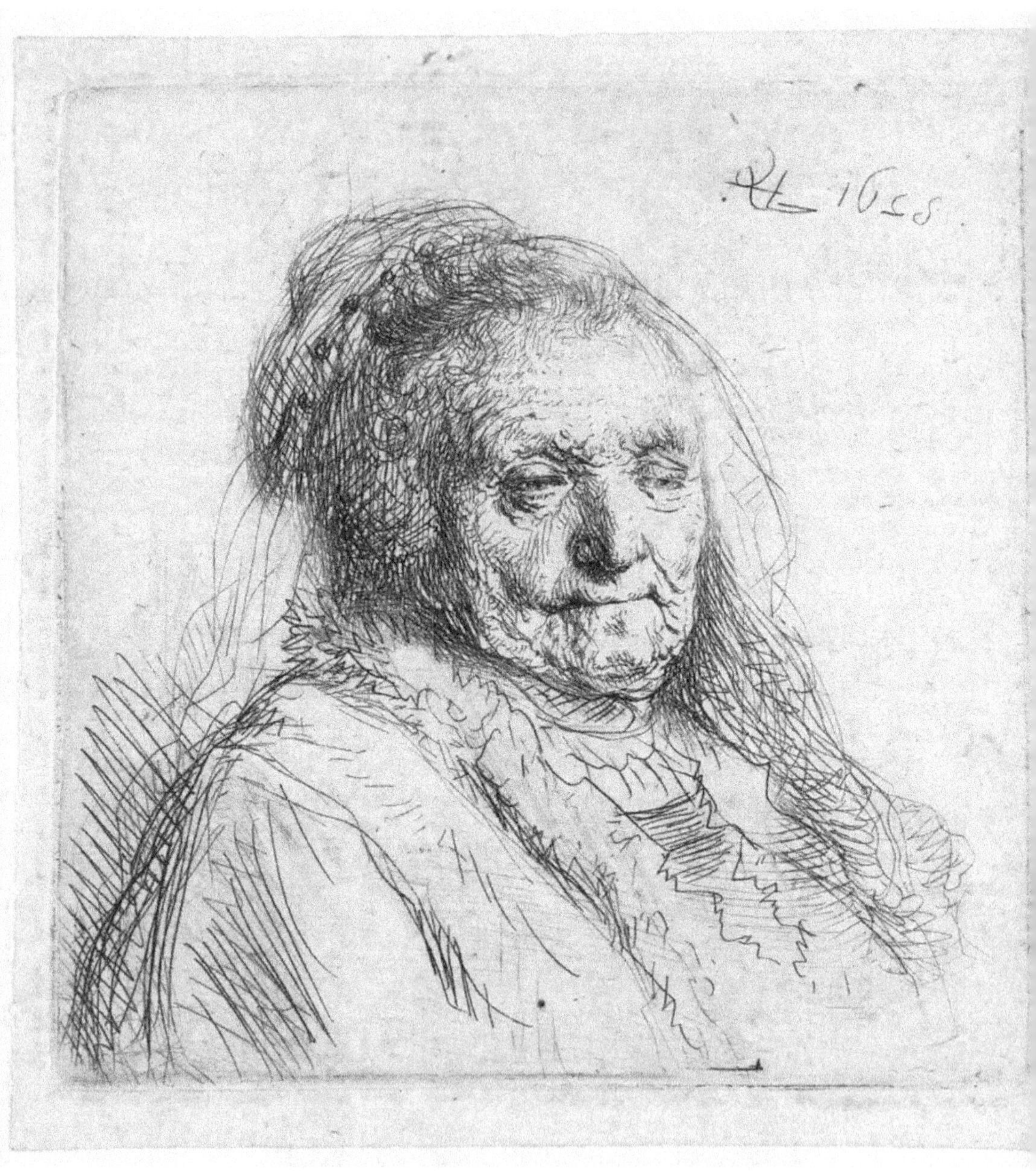

Rembrandt, Mother, 1628, Rijksmuseum, Amsterdam

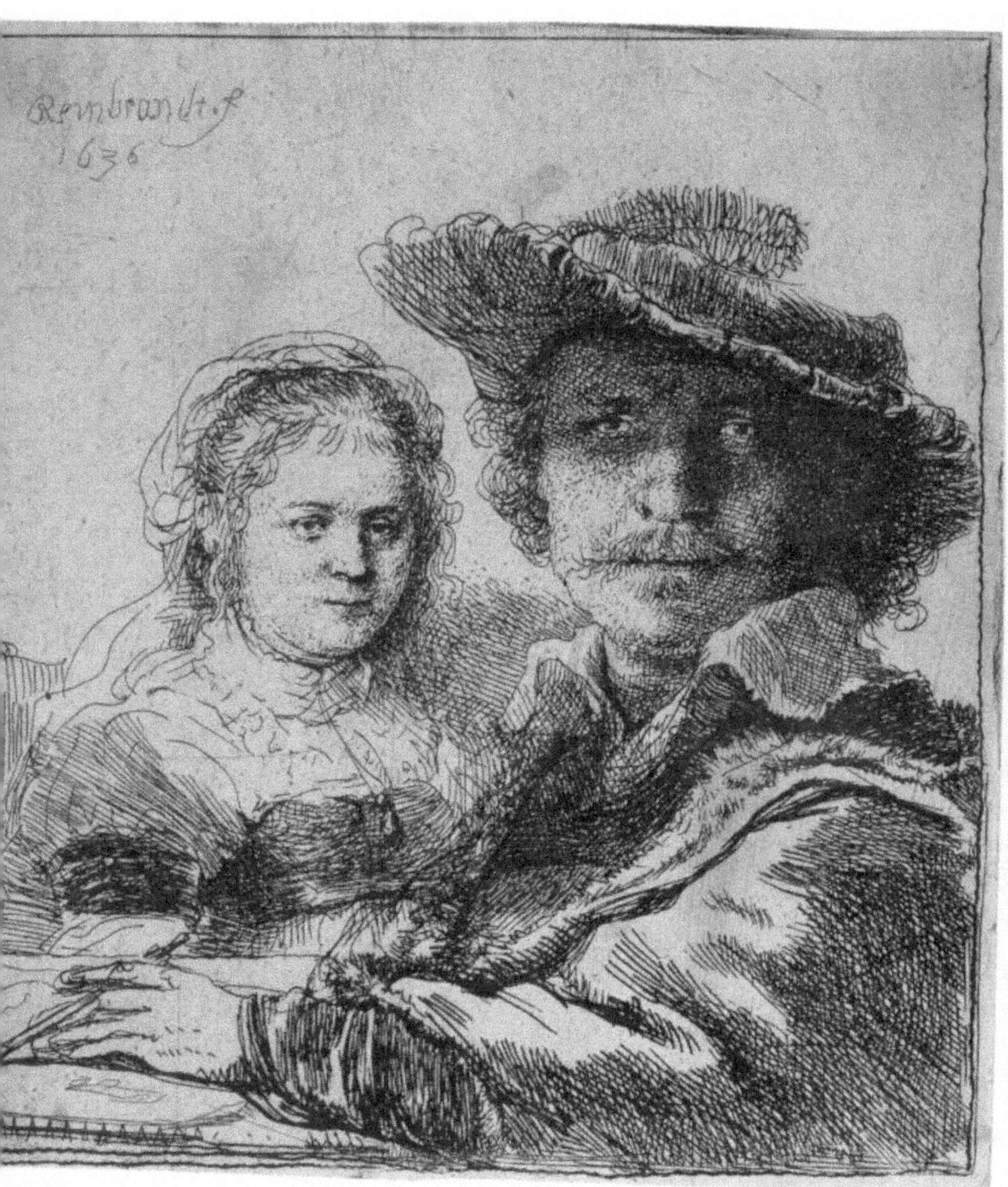

Rembrandt, Self-Portrait With Saskia, 1636, Hermitage Museum

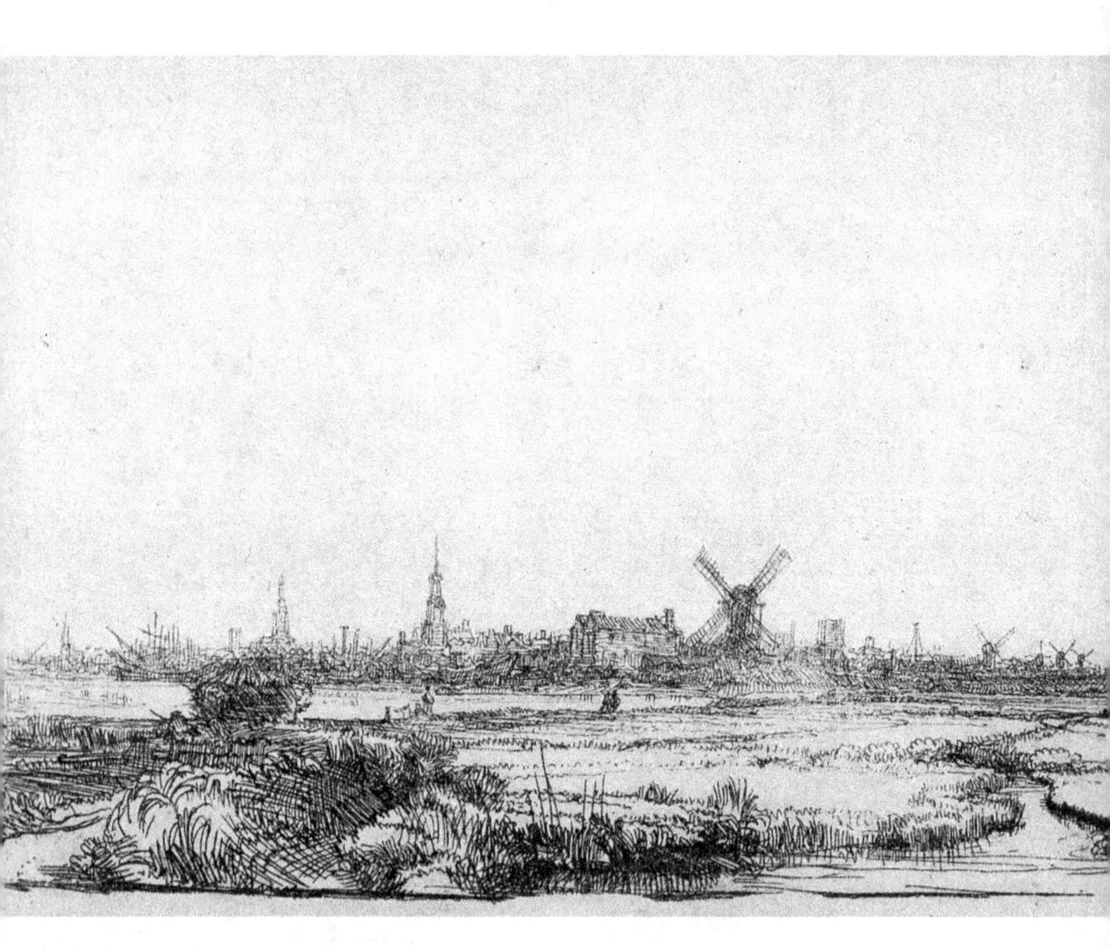

Rembrandt, Amsterdam, c. 1640

CRESCENT MOON PUBLISHING

web: www.crmoon.com e-mail: cresmopub@yahoo.co.uk

ARTS, PAINTING, SCULPTURE

The Art of Andy Goldsworthy
Andy Goldsworthy: Touching Nature
Andy Goldsworthy in Close-Up
Andy Goldsworthy: Pocket Guide
Andy Goldsworthy In America

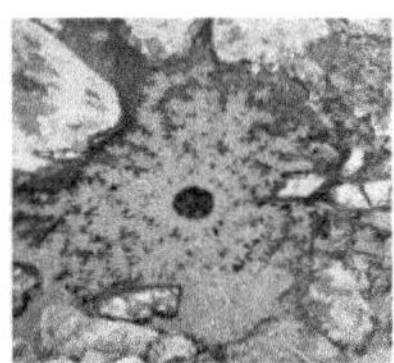

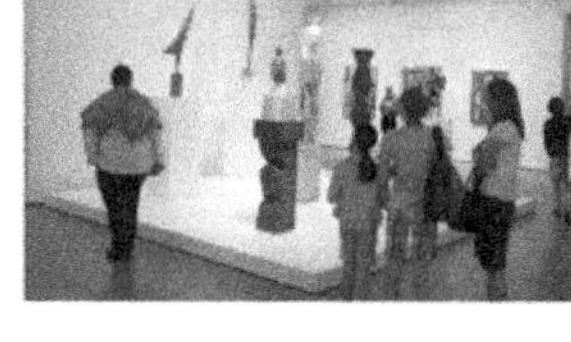

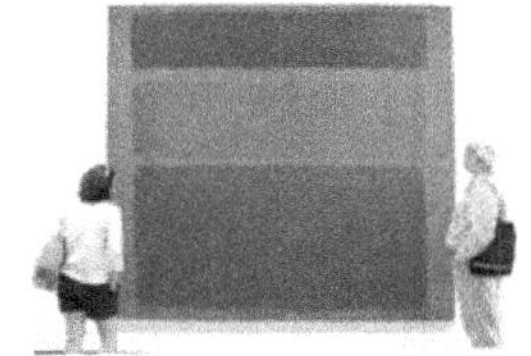

Land Art: A Complete Guide
The Art of Richard Long
Richard Long: Pocket Guide
Land Art In the UK
Land Art in Close-Up
Land Art In the U.S.A.
Land Art: Pocket Guide
Installation Art in Close-Up
Minimal Art and Artists In the 1960s and After
Colourfield Painting
Land Art DVD, TV documentary
Andy Goldsworthy DVD, TV documentary
The Erotic Object: Sexuality in Sculpture From Prehistory to the Present Day
Sex in Art: Pornography and Pleasure in Painting and Sculpture
Postwar Art
Sacred Gardens: The Garden in Myth, Religion and Art
Glorification: Religious Abstraction in Renaissance and 20th Century Art
Early Netherlandish Painting
Leonardo da Vinci
Piero della Francesca
Giovanni Bellini
Fra Angelico: Art and Religion in the Renaissance
Mark Rothko: The Art of Transcendence
Frank Stella: American Abstract Artist
Jasper Johns
Brice Marden
Alison Wilding: The Embrace of Sculpture
Vincent van Gogh: Visionary Landscapes
Eric Gill: Nuptials of God
Constantin Brancusi: Sculpting the Essence of Things
Max Beckmann
Caravaggio
Gustave Moreau
Egon Schiele: Sex and Death In Purple Stockings
Delizioso Fotografico Fervore: Works In Process 1
Sacro Cuore: Works In Process 2
The Light Eternal: J.M.W. Turner
The Madonna Glorified: Karen Arthurs

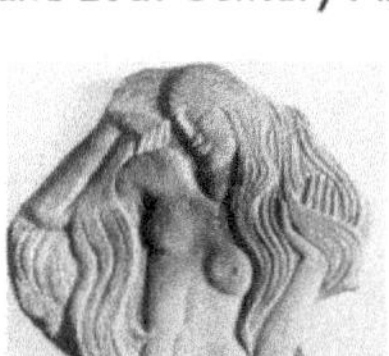

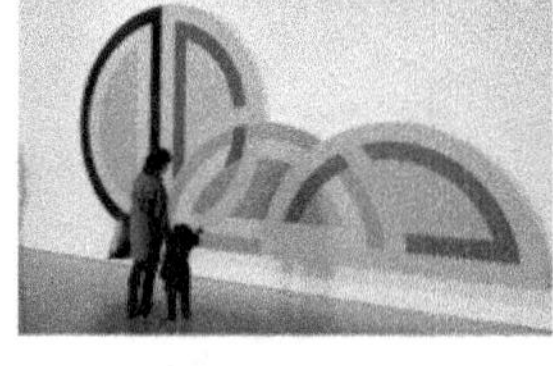

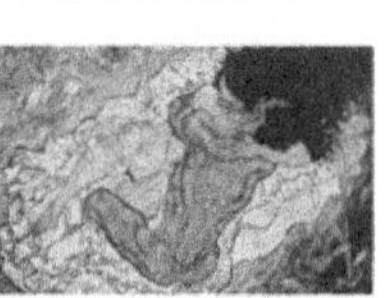

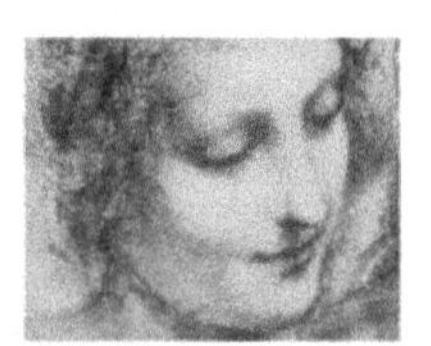

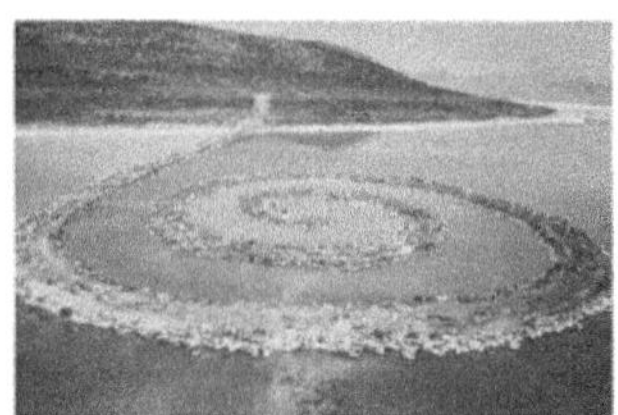

LITERATURE

J.R.R. Tolkien: The Books, The Films, The Whole Cultural Phenomenon
J.R.R. Tolkien: Pocket Guide
Tolkien's Heroic Quest
The *Earthsea* Books of Ursula Le Guin
Beauties, Beasts and Enchantment: Classic French Fairy Tales
German Popular Stories by the Brothers Grimm
Philip Pullman and *His Dark Materials*
Sexing Hardy: Thomas Hardy and Feminism
Thomas Hardy's *Tess of the d'Urbervilles* 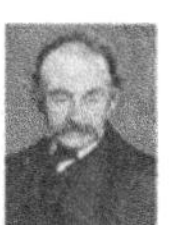
Thomas Hardy's *Jude the Obscure*
Thomas Hardy: The Tragic Novels
Love and Tragedy: Thomas Hardy
The Poetry of Landscape in Hardy
Wessex Revisited: Thomas Hardy and John Cowper Powys
Wolfgang Iser: Essays and Interviews 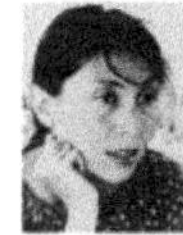
Petrarch, Dante and the Troubadours
Maurice Sendak and the Art of Children's Book Illustration
Andrea Dworkin
Cixous, Irigaray, Kristeva: The *Jouissance* of French Feminism
Julia Kristeva: Art, Love, Melancholy, Philosophy, Semiotics and Psychoanalysis
Hélene Cixous I Love You: The *Jouissance* of Writing
Luce Irigaray: Lips, Kissing, and the Politics of Sexual Difference
Peter Redgrove: Here Comes the Flood
Peter Redgrove: Sex-Magic-Poetry-Cornwall
Lawrence Durrell: Between Love and Death, East and West
Love, Culture & Poetry: Lawrence Durrell 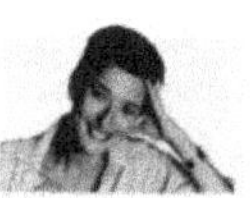
Cavafy: Anatomy of a Soul
German Romantic Poetry: Goethe, Novalis, Heine, Hölderlin
Feminism and Shakespeare
Shakespeare: Love, Poetry & Magic 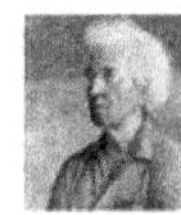
The Passion of D.H. Lawrence
D.H. Lawrence: Symbolic Landscapes 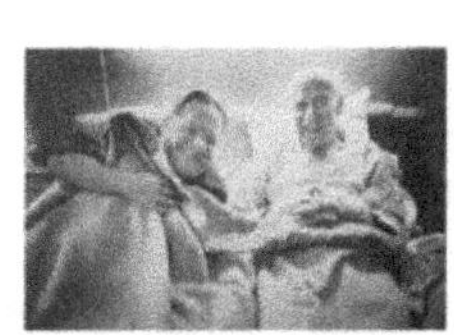
D.H. Lawrence: Infinite Sensual Violence
Rimbaud: Arthur Rimbaud and the Magic of Poetry
The Ecstasies of John Cowper Powys
Sensualism and Mythology: The Wessex Novels of John Cowper Powys
Amorous Life: John Cowper Powys and the Manifestation of Affectivity (H.W. Fawkner)
Postmodern Powys: New Essays on John Cowper Powys (Joe Boulter)
Rethinking Powys: Critical Essays on John Cowper Powys
Paul Bowles & Bernardo Bertolucci
Rainer Maria Rilke 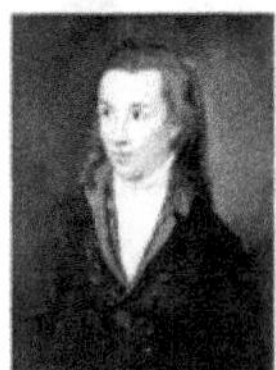
Joseph Conrad: *Heart of Darkness* 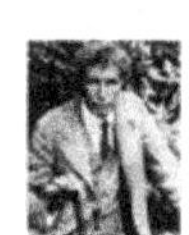
In the Dim Void: Samuel Beckett
Samuel Beckett Goes into the Silence
André Gide: Fiction and Fervour
Jackie Collins and the Blockbuster Novel
Blinded By Her Light: The Love-Poetry of Robert Graves
The Passion of Colours: Travels In Mediterranean Lands
Poetic Forms

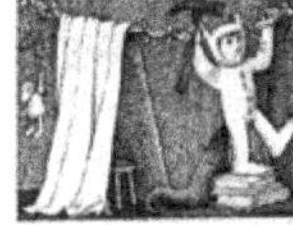
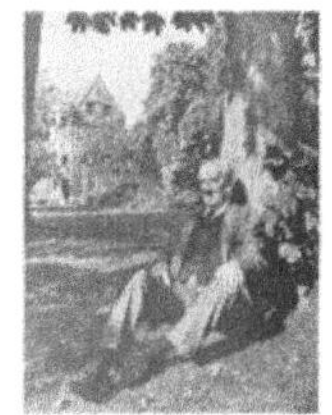

POETRY

Ursula Le Guin: Walking In Cornwall
Peter Redgrove: Here Comes The Flood
Peter Redgrove: Sex-Magic-Poetry-Cornwall
Dante: Selections From the Vita Nuova
Petrarch, Dante and the Troubadours
William Shakespeare: Sonnets
William Shakespeare: Complete Poems
Blinded By Her Light: The Love-Poetry of Robert Graves
Emily Dickinson: Selected Poems
Emily Brontë: Poems
Thomas Hardy: Selected Poems
Percy Bysshe Shelley: Poems
John Keats: Selected Poems
Joh n Keats: Poems of 1820
D.H. Lawrence: Selected Poems
Edmund Spenser: Poems
Edmund Spenser: Amoretti
John Donne: Poems
Henry Vaughan: Poems
Sir Thomas Wyatt: Poems
Robert Herrick: Selected Poems
Rilke: Space, Essence and Angels in the Poetry of Rainer Maria Rilke
Rainer Maria Rilke: Selected Poems
Friedrich Hölderlin: Selected Poems
Arseny Tarkovsky: Selected Poems
Arthur Rimbaud: Selected Poems
Arthur Rimbaud: A Season in Hell
Arthur Rimbaud and the Magic of Poetry
Novalis: Hymns To the Night
German Romantic Poetry
Paul Verlaine: Selected Poems
Elizaethan Sonnet Cycles
D.J. Enright: By-Blows
Jeremy Reed: Brigitte's Blue Heart
Jeremy Reed: Claudia Schiffer's Red Shoes
Gorgeous Little Orpheus
Radiance: New Poems
Crescent Moon Book of Nature Poetry
Crescent Moon Book of Love Poetry
Crescent Moon Book of Mystical Poetry
Crescent Moon Book of Elizabethan Love Poetry
Crescent Moon Book of Metaphysical Poetry
Crescent Moon Book of Romantic Poetry
Pagan America: New American Poetry

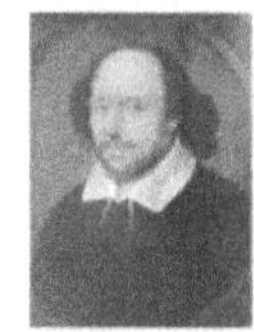
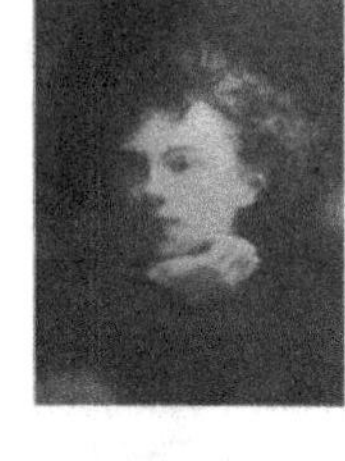
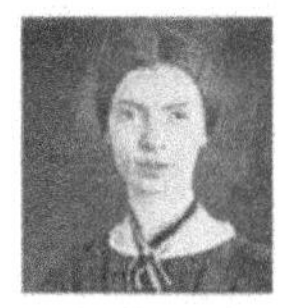
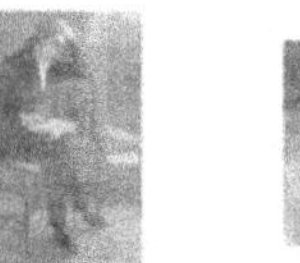
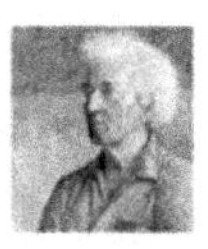
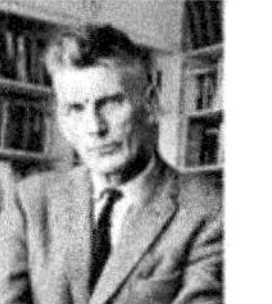
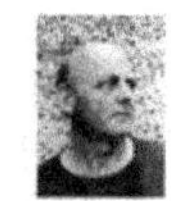
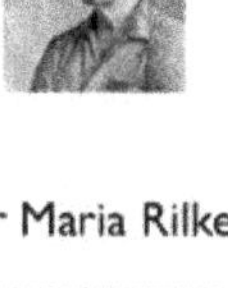
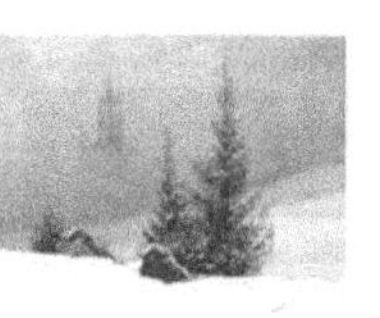
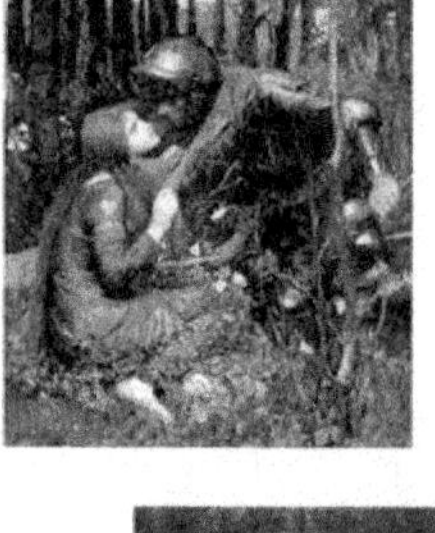
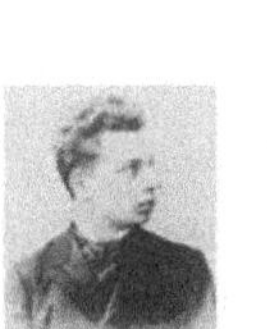
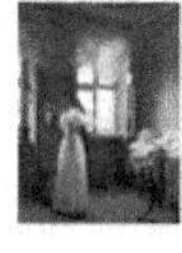
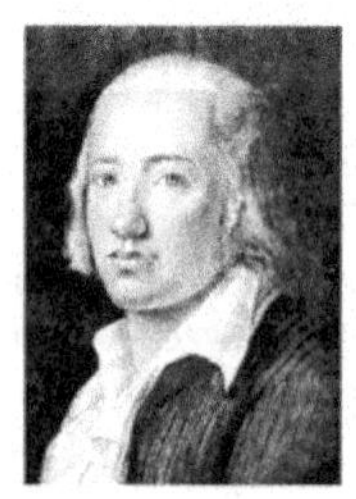
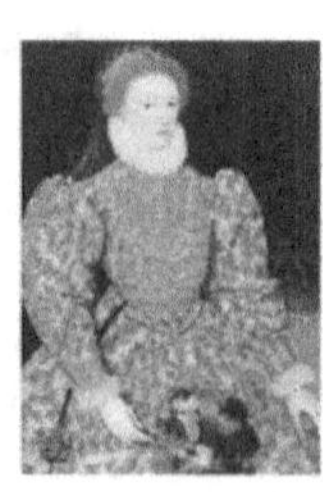

MEDIA, CINEMA, FEMINISM and CULTURAL STUDIES

J.R.R. Tolkien: The Books, The Films, The Whole Cultural Phenomenon
J.R.R. Tolkien: Pocket Guide
The *Lord of the Rings* Movies: Pocket Guide
The Cinema of Hayao Miyazaki
Hayao Miyazaki: *Princess Mononoke*: Pocket Movie Guide
Hayao Miyazaki: *Spirited Away*: Pocket Movie Guide
Tim Burton : Hallowe'en For Hollywood
Ken Russell
Ken Russell: *Tommy*: Pocket Movie Guide
The Ghost Dance: The Origins of Religion
The Peyote Cult

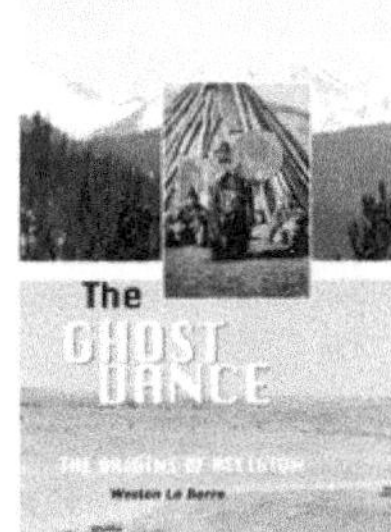
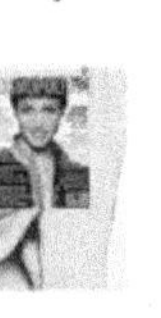

Cixous, Irigaray, Kristeva: The *Jouissance* of French Feminism
Julia Kristeva: Art, Love, Melancholy, Philosophy, Semiotics and Psychoanalysis
Luce Irigaray: Lips, Kissing, and the Politics of Sexual Difference
Hélène Cixous I Love You: The *Jouissance* of Writing
Andrea Dworkin
'Cosmo Woman': The World of Women's Magazines
Women in Pop Music
HomeGround: The Kate Bush Anthology
Discovering the Goddess (Geoffrey Ashe)
The Poetry of Cinema
The Sacred Cinema of Andrei Tarkovsky
Andrei Tarkovsky: Pocket Guide
Andrei Tarkovsky: *Mirror*: Pocket Movie Guide
Andrei Tarkovsky: *The Sacrifice*: Pocket Movie Guide
Walerian Borowczyk: Cinema of Erotic Dreams
Jean-Luc Godard: The Passion of Cinema
Jean-Luc Godard: *Hail Mary*: Pocket Movie Guide
Jean-Luc Godard: *Contempt*: Pocket Movie Guide
Jean-Luc Godard: *Pierrot le Fou*: Pocket Movie Guide
John Hughes and Eighties Cinema
Ferris Bueller's Day Off: Pocket Movie Guide
Jean-Luc Godard: Pocket Guide
The Cinema of Richard Linklater
Liv Tyler: Star In Ascendance
Blade Runner and the Films of Philip K. Dick
Paul Bowles and Bernardo Bertolucci
Media Hell: Radio, TV and the Press
An Open Letter to the BBC
Detonation Britain: Nuclear War in the UK
Feminism and Shakespeare
Wild Zones: Pornography, Art and Feminism
Sex in Art: Pornography and Pleasure in Painting and Sculpture
Sexing Hardy: Thomas Hardy and Feminism

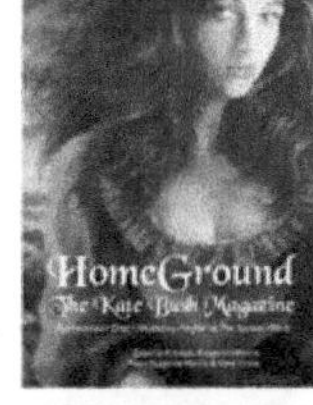
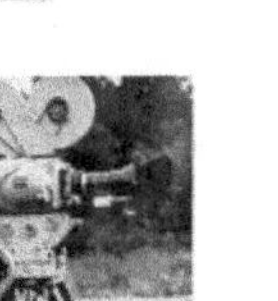
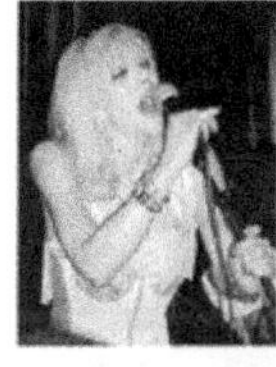
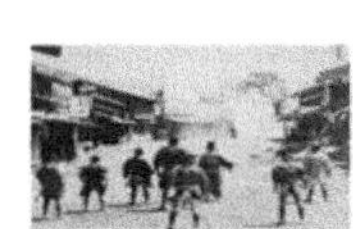
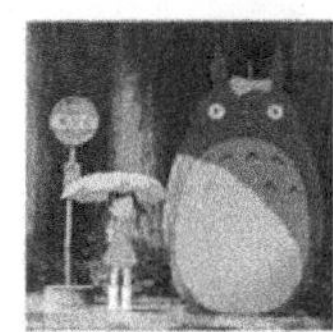
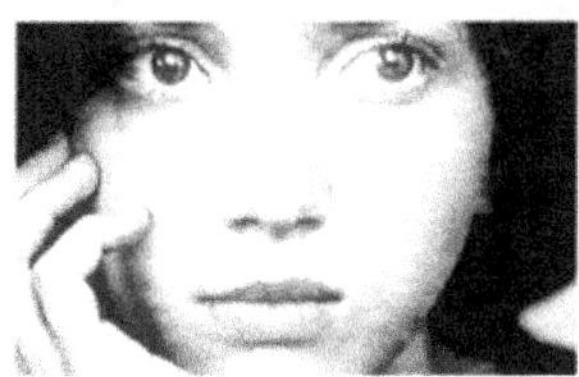

The Light Eternal is a model monograph, an exemplary job. The subject matter of the book is beautifully organised and dead on beam. (Lawrence Durrell)

It is amazing for me to see my work treated with such passion and respect. (Andrea Dworkin)

CRESCENT MOON PUBLISHING
P.O. Box 1312, Maidstone, Kent, ME14 5XU, Great Britain. www.crmoon.com

cresmopub@yahoo.co.uk   www.crescentmoon.org.uk
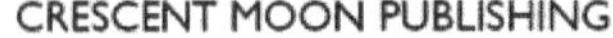